The Loss of a Pet

"Old Drum Memorial." The bronze plaque beneath the statue contains the entire text of a speech by the late Senator Vest of Missouri. In the 1870 trial of a man from Warrensburg, who had wantonly shot a neighbor's dog, Vest asked $200 in damages. After this brief but effective speech, the jury deliberated only two minutes and awarded the plaintiff $500.

Courtesy, City of Warrensburg, MO

The Loss
of a Pet

Wallace Sife, Ph.D.

HOWELL
BOOK HOUSE
New York

Maxwell Macmillan Canada
Toronto

Maxwell Macmillan International
New York   Oxford   Singapore   Sydney

Howell Book House
Macmillan Publishing Company
866 Third Avenue
New York, NY 10022

Maxwell Macmillan Canada, Inc.
1200 Eglinton Avenue East
Suite 200
Don Mills, Ontario M3C 3N1

Macmillan Publishing Company is part of the Maxwell Communication Group of Companies.

Library of Congress Cataloging-in-Publication Data

Sife, Wallace.
    The loss of a pet/Wallace Sife.
      p.   cm.
    ISBN 0-87605-625-7
    1. Pet owners—Psychology.   2. Pets—Death—Psychological aspects.
    3. Bereavement—Psychological aspects.   I. Title.
    SF411.47.S54   1993
    155.9'37—dc20   92–31092
                                                  CIP

Macmillan books are available at special discounts for bulk purchases for sales promotions, premiums, fund-raising, or educational use. For details, contact:

Special Sales Director
Macmillan Publishing Company
866 Third Avenue
New York, NY 10022

10 9 8 7 6 5 4 3 2

Printed in the United States of America

To peace and permanence, in the loving memory of my pal,
Dachshund Edel Meister, MS, CD (1979–1987),
and all his soul mates who were beloved,
and the good people who mourn our common loss.

A TRIBUTE TO THE DOG

By Senator George Graham Vest

A speech made by the late Senator Vest of Missouri in the trial of a man at Warrensburg, who had wantonly shot a dog belonging to a neighbor. Mr. Vest represened the plaintiff, who demanded $200 damages. As a result of the speech, the jury after two minutes deliberation awarded the plaintiff $500.

"Gentlemen of the Jury: The best friend a man has in this world may turn against him and become his enemy. His son or daughter that he has reared with loving care may prove ungrateful. Those who are nearest and dearest to us, those whom we trust with our happiness and our good name, may become traitors to their faith. The money that a man has, he may lose. It flies away from him, perhaps when he needs it the most. A man's reputation may be sacrificed in a moment of ill-considered action. The people who are prone to fall on their knees to do us honor when success is with us may be the first to throw the stone of malice when failure settles its cloud upon our heads. The one absolutely unselfish friend that a man can have in this selfish world, the one that never deserts him and the one that never proves ungrateful or treacherous is his dog.

"Gentlemen of the Jury, a man's dog stands by him in prosperity and in poverty, in health and in sickness. He will sleep on the cold ground, where the wintry winds blow and the snow drives fiercely, if only he may be near his master's side. He will kiss the hand that has no food to offer, he will lick the wounds and sores that come in encounters with the roughness of the world. He guards the sleep of his pauper master as if he were a prince. When all other friends desert he remains. When riches take wings and reputation falls to pieces, he is as constant in his love as the sun in its journey through the heavens. If fortune drives the master forth an outcast in the world, friendless and homeless, the faithful dog asks no higher privilege than that of accompanying him to guard against danger, to fight against his enemies, and when the last scene of all comes, and death takes the master in its embrace and his body is laid away in the cold ground, no matter if all other friends pursue their way, there by his graveside will the noble dog be found, his head between his paws, his eyes sad but open in alert watchfulness, faithful and true even to death.

Courtesy of *The Daily Star-Journal*
Warrensburg, MO.
Inscribed on the Old Drum Memorial
Warrensburg, MO
1870

Contents

Foreword

T HE FIRST TIME I met Dr. Sife, it was to discuss his professional interest in pet loss counseling. He recognized the power of pet-person relationships and felt society had paid far too little attention to the pain that people experience when these relationships end. He wanted to join the small group of mental health professionals caring for the bereaved companions of pets who had died.

The next time I met Dr. Sife, he had become one of the bereaved. The sudden death of his dog, Edel Meister, prompted him to join the Animal Medical Center's Pet Loss Support Group, the first ongoing service of its kind.

In the midst of his own sorrow, Dr. Sife found the strength to offer consolation to others who came to the group. Whether their losses were recent or many months old, he drew on his own experience to help others understand what they were feeling. He began to talk about writing a book that would be therapeutic and healing for others. *The Loss of a Pet* is that book.

Written from the perspective of a fellow mourner, while drawing on his training and experience as a psychologist, *The Loss of a Pet* supports the right of those people whose companion animals have died to feel whatever is natural for them. Sadly, many who are grieving have their pain increased by the awkwardness or apathy of friends and family. Dr. Sife describes how to protect oneself from additional hurt, while remaining open to any attempts, no matter how halting, to comfort.

People who have lost pets, and those around them, wonder why attachment and grief are so strong. Both groups question at what point these feelings become extreme, potentially harmful. Wallace Sife explains how companion animals offer a rich but safe kind of interaction. At the same time he offers a few examples from his professional practice.

Dr. Sife does more than describe feelings of grief and explain their origin; he suggests concrete steps to deal with the confusing and unpleasant sensations that go hand-in-hand with these feelings. Chapter 5 is a good example. First he ties anger, a normal stage of bereavement, to frustration at lack of control. He then outlines a technique for handling anger without hurting oneself or others. He suggests writing down all the reasons to be angry, then he recommends discussing these with trusted friends, practicing the perspective of each person involved.

The Loss of a Pet is a personal book that reflects Wallace Sife's unique views on pet loss. His passionate commitment to personal growth and happiness underscores his call to accept reality and let go of the past. Professional readers will find he has added a different dimension to old concepts. His caring for the relief of suffering shines through the entire work. In *The Loss of a Pet* he has taken his own advice, to create a living memorial to a very special dog.

Susan Phillips Cohen, MSW
Director of Counseling
Animal Medical Center
New York City

Board of Directors
Delta Society

Introduction

Grief must have a purpose, otherwise it is meaningless and destructive.

IF YOU ARE a very special kind of person who grieves deeply for the loss of a beloved pet, this book is written for you. What is presented in these pages will help you realize that you are not alone. Others have suffered the same anguish from the death of a cherished animal. What we have learned about this inevitable yet tragic experience can help you. It will teach you about this exceptionally painful and mystifying impact on your life. The shock of bereavement is one of the most profound emotional traumas we can experience.

Human beings are creatures of habit and patterns. We find security in routines and established orders. Our individual personalities become powerful subconscious patterns for our behaviors. Some of these are ingrained while we are very young. Others we create, and add to our lives later.

Living with a beloved pet for an extended part of our lives produces new patterns. All of us lovingly configure our life-styles around this cherished adopted family member. We become accustomed to the routines. Our companionship is taken for granted, and we live with it as if it will never end. But it does. Suddenly it is gone. The resultant shock is normal.

The emotional reaction to the death of a pet is determined by our degree of involvement with that animal. This book is concerned with people in great emotional distress. Judgmentalism has no place, but is foisted on us by those who are generally insensitive or threatened by the mourning for a pet. These critics lack a basic sense of tolerance or respect for others. The grief we feel in pet bereavement is belittled even more by indifference in a society where humane animal rights and laws still are nearly impossible to enforce. Those persons feel that others should not suffer real bereavement for a pet, as an animal "can always be replaced." Their harsh responses, for whatever reasons, should not become your problem, especially at this very painful and vulnerable time of loss in your own life.

Unfortunately, there are not enough people who can comprehend our grief and we must learn to readjust our relationships with others, as a defensive posture. We must also be cautious and avoid angry overreactions, which are more easily experienced now, but may later be regretted. Those of us who mourn the death of a pet are most often more generous in our expressions of care and concern for others. And we are more vulnerable, too.

The mourning for a pet can be far more intense than for a human. This will be explained in more detail in a later chapter. The pain you are experiencing now is very real, and possibly debilitating. You are actually mourning the death of a very close member of your immediate family, nothing less!

Be grateful for any attempts by others, however awkward, to ease your pain. But don't give in to any subtle pressure to belittle your grief. You must learn to make this important distinction.

Death, in general, is a subject that most people are very uncomfortable with. Discussion on the subject is awkward or even impossible. People don't know how to discuss it without embarrassment, evasion or pretense. Euphemisms generally attempt to provide evasive expressions for more specific terms and ideas. You may discover that the passing of your cherished companion pet is too difficult or distressing for some people to comprehend or even be tolerant about.

Historically, tradition and religion have avoided the subject of pet death, leaving the full responsibility and burden solely up to the confused, lonely and distraught mourner of a beloved animal friend. Up until very recently each person suffered alone. Now, we have become an acknowledged community within our ever-changing society.

Individual pastoral counseling in this context, if it can be found, may offer some help. But the death of animals is not officially acknowledged by most of the world's major religions. That seems to be justified by the general feeling that there is more than enough difficulty in dealing with human death to get involved with our problem. There are many who believe the concept of a soul includes any sentient being that is endowed with love. In the future, official religious agreement probably will be adjusted to this belief. This book presents an unusual chapter, partly composed of brief articles by religious leaders, attempting to address the rising problem of the death of pets. The spiritual needs and considerations of humanity are changing with our socioeconomic evolution. Pets have become more significant, loved members of most households. Aside from veterinary care, a multibillion-dollar business now caters to the needs and care of pets in the United States alone.

Dynamic changes in contemporary civilization are causing the disappearance of the extended household, and a decrease in family size. Along with a very rapidly growing population, there are now more single, divorced and widowed people than ever before. This new element of our population keeps more pets than any other in history. Lonely people, in particular, are well aware of the wonderful love and therapeutic effects companion animals have on us.

Pets may serve as the only safe "attachment figures" in the lives of many. Many times these pet owners are sensitive souls who have suffered inadequate parenting or an unsupportive marriage. Emotionally battered people are very often the most dependent of pet owners, and may grieve the hardest.

In many ways, the pet becomes an extension of our own personalities. It represents that secretly held, half-formed image of our purest self. In a hard world this may be the only outlet that can represent our inner love and vulnerability. Without a pet, this important expression may never be made. So there should be little wonder at the intensity of grief and bereavement for such a death.

Unconsciously, we weep for ourselves as well. Also, the pet is a loving soul, and we mourn it accordingly. Its life has taken it to that other realm. Someday we will be there also.

Who has not experienced that special sense of awareness and greeting, when we put the key in the lock and open the door? Just coming home is a major event. We had become so used to anticipating our pet's welcome, from a meow or so to a tail-thumping salute. Now it is silent. But the pet's presence still seems everywhere. We now live in the echoes of the loving patterns that became our way of life.

Too often those we rely on most let us down during this grief. At times we are fortunate to find caring, supportive people— usually other pet owners who can share our feelings and responses. But this is too rare. Also, there have been far too few things published in any of the mass media on this subject. This author has been through the worst of it, and learned the hard way, all too alone. My own personal pain and needs, and those of my many patients, have made the writing of this book necessary. I hope it gives you what you need to help yourself through your mourning for your beloved pet.

1

The Human-Pet Bond

"Everything that lives, lives not alone nor for itself."
—William Blake

THE HUMAN-PET BOND is one that goes far back into the dim prehistoric times. Some cave drawings depict dogs joining in the hunt, as well as the camp and around the fire—sharing life space with our earliest of ancestors. That primitive bonding was no accident or act of frivolity, but a natural interaction, serving the basic needs of both humans and animals. This included mutual protection and companionship, as well as improved herding and hunting.

After countless thousands of years, this common bond became very specialized, according to the comforts and changing needs of civilization. Beyond working dogs, we now keep companion animals of all kinds for the pure pleasure of their company. They enrich our lives in many different ways, and can serve as a playful pal or best friend, and even a surrogate child.

There is a basic need for humans to give love and nurture. This is best demonstrated by the natural tendency in children to care for their dolls and toy animals. Even some adults still enjoy the pleasure of owning these. The human baby has an inherent love of soft, cuddly things. They are made into fantasy pals, and treated with great personal care and affection. When we grow up, this loving human instinct is usually transferred to more traditional objects of affection. But this instinct for taking care of the cuddly animal or baby substitute is always with us. Thus, the pet serves a very important purpose in our humanity.

The pleasures derived from the keeping of a companion animal go beyond any objective comments that can be listed here. Pets give us innocent dependence, companionship and love. Above all, a pet is totally accepting and nonjudgmental. With time, the unique emotional bonding between the pet and the owner intensifies for each. This becomes a wonderful coupling that can't be compared to any other kind of relationship. Our pets become whatever we want them to in our lives, and never seem to fail us. We judge ourselves by them. Their companionship gives us added stability and purpose, and a sense of personal enrichment that defies description.

A RELATIONSHIP OF MUTUAL BENEFIT

The bond we develop with pets is as wonderful and rewarding as it is fascinating and practical. This is an active reaching out and sharing of life with another living being, who happens not to be human. It offers us a chance to share and express our pure selves, without need to ever defend our actions or feelings. Pets, as we have come to call them, give us our greatest opportunities to express love, without ever having to worry about being judged or rejected. They give us back a devotion that is unmatched by any other relationships, in a very private bond. Pets give us an oasis of unqualified love and acceptance in an otherwise demanding and critical world. Their obedience and respect give us an increased sense of self-worth, adding new meaning to our lives. In return, we elevate them to positions of great personal value.

"Faithful and Constant Companions"
Courtesy, Hartsdale Canine Cemetery, Inc.

In memory of a precious cat.   *Courtesy, Abbey Glen Pet Memorial Park*

This can make us more vulnerable, however, in our bereavement when our pets die.

We touch and caress our pets freely, and they reward us by reassuring us in many ways that they find pleasure in this. Touching affords us an unrestrained outlet for our love and affection. This action is very enriching emotionally. Yet it is an expression that is still highly guarded in most other social expressions. This simple tactile contact has been proven to be of significant medical and psychological benefit as well. Blood pressure is reduced, the heartbeat is improved, resistance is heightened and tension is eased, among other tangible benefits. Just from stroking our pets!

This relationship has a dimension that transcends relationships between people, as wonderful as they can be. We open up completely to pets, and receive an inner sense of joy and strength at being so adored in return.

So often it has been said that pets can be truer friends than people. That is because they are never critical, and therefore allow us to blossom emotionally in ways that would not be possble or appropriate with fellow humans. We make our pets our secret sharers, to levels of security beyond what is often entrusted to friends, family or even spouses.

Sometimes these expressions of our very private selves are taken out of proportion to what is safe or normal. There are pet lovers who have forsaken some or much of their interhuman relationships for this sense of love and security. They can isolate themselves with their pets from the rest of the world, which may seem too threatening, painful or dangerous. That can prove very unhealthy in the long run. And there are many who live lives of quiet desperation, who develop too strong a dependency on a pet for supportiveness in different kinds of stressful social situations.

Frequently, when there is a strong conflict between two family members, one of them will turn to the pet for comfort and love, for a sense of supportiveness, which they need. This dependent relationship becomes very personal and secret. With time, it grows in magnitude if the discord is not resolved.

When the pet dies it leaves a terrible void in the dependent person's life. If the death is sudden, then the shock is usually very intense. If the death has been more gradual, despair and depression usually follow, and are more pronounced.

It is a wonderful experience to love and care for a pet. But we must love ourselves as well as our pets, in order to survive and continue to lead productive lives.

We must not lose sight of our being part of a larger social structure that cannot be denied. Aside from civic responsibility, we have a humane one to ourselves, to grow and prosper, and find love within the community of man. The lonely person who despairs of finding love and being needed often turns to pets for this outlet. That is all well and good, but it should not become an escape or substitute, or offer an emotional buffer that isolates us from our needs for human companionship. With the inevitable death of the pet, this personal oasis evaporates, and we have made ourselves very vulnerable to extremes of loneliness, grief and bereavement.

HUMAN/ANIMAL DEPENDENCY

Almost without exception, grief responses are most extreme when the bereaved has very few or no significantly close companions. In a sort of vicious cycle, the love for a pet becomes all the more intense to compensate for this. As pet owners, we can unwittingly set ourselves up for disaster, using this relationship as a retreat from the pain and loneliness of everyday coping. It becomes a safe cocoon, with the rest of the world left outside. But reality always catches up with us. Death always comes.

The relationships we develop with our pets define the quality and style of our lives. Pets are what we make them, and we become products of this relationship. We can love them as pets, or as surrogate children, or as replacements for other people. We can dote on them, squandering our precious life energies and time, or we can treat them as joyful companions in our own trek through life. That is our choice.

One of the most dramatic cases I ever treated was that of a painfully shy and sensitive young woman in her thirties, whose small dog was really her best friend. They were inseparable. When dating, she occasionally brought the dog along. Because this woman could not find a suitable mate, she developed an emotional dependency on her pet, which intensified with time. Naturally, the dog didn't truly express opinions or supportiveness, but its unqualified love and absolute faithfulness were interpreted as such. It became a sort of alter ego with the woman's emotional needs and fantasies.

This situation developed into one where the dog was no longer just an adoring, loving pet. In her mind it became a symbol of all the goodness she could not find in a friend or mate for herself. This became a prescription for personal disaster. Eventually, the dog died, as all living things must, and the woman became an emotional basket case. Her only love was her deceased pet and a dream.

I use this example because we all project certain human values on our beloved animal companions. To some degree, we each must endure some of the same grief this lonely, loving woman created for herself in bereavement. But when we tinker with reality, it must eventually get back at us.

The bond between humans and pets has changed dramatically, from biblical through modern times. Today, they are rarely used any longer as working animals, as in herding or hunting. At this time, a desire for the special company of a pet is all the justification we need. The most important function that animal companionship now serves is psychological. The pet's presence is comforting and full of love. It reinforces the ego-strength and self-image of its master. Thus, the evolving human-pet bond has become a modern phenomenon.

Companion animal care and pet food now have developed into the basis for a staggering multibillion-dollar industry in the United States alone. The acceptance and awareness of pets is becoming universal. It also follows that the death care of pets also is becoming increasingly recognized and practiced. This, too, is starting to boom as a big business. A scandal involving flagrant abuse of mass animal burials in a pet cemetery on Long Island,

10

New York, has illustrated just how deeply pet owners love their companion animals.

IT'S OK TO MOURN FOR A PET

In our society males have a much more difficult time during the bereavement period. They have been conditioned and admonished by a lifetime of customs and cultural mores that it is not manly to cry, even in private. Fortunately, we are gaining insight into this behavior. Ours is an age of beginning enlightenment on many levels, as never before in history.

With the human-pet bond growing so pervasive and strong in recent times, we have come to a changing point in human behavior. Pet bereavement and its related problems are emerging as a new social phenomenon of our Western culture. The growing visibility of vast pet-related industries is causing a new public awareness of some of the ramifications of this hitherto little-understood bond.

Yet, many insensitive or non-pet-oriented people still have absolutely no concept of the human-pet bond. Too often the bereft pet owner is criticized or dismissed, like a foolish person. In most cases the reasons for this kind of discrimination lie in ignorance and deep-rooted psychological inadequacy. But these people can still upset us, even though their type is decreasing in numbers, and they are actually expressing their own problems, not ours.

We are most vulnerable when we are in mourning. With increasing awareness and recognition, the easy talk and criticism that was once so prevalent is now on the wane. But the battles and skirmishes are not yet over.

This bond is a very special relationship. The sharing between people and pets offers many private and precious moments together. They are as unique as they are intensely personal and gratifying. Such mutual love is its own greatest justification for us to ever find joy in our pets, as well as ourselves. Children have their security blankets; we have our pets.

We get much love and delight from them in life, and grieve

deeply when they die. Because of the unique enhancement they give to our lives, they become a treasured part of us forever. When a pet's life ends, more dies than just one beloved companion animal. Pets are made into a living symbol of each person's best feelings and thoughts. Thus, a part of each of us dies also, but can be reborn as we pick up our emotional pieces and move on. It is in our nature to believe that our spirits will reunite in a better way when we eventually follow them.

We honor and respect the human-pet bond as we admire and value the humans and the pet animals.

2

Responsibility

"He prayeth well who loveth well both man and bird and beast."

—Samuel Taylor Coleridge

WHEN WE MAKE that wonderful decision to have a pet, we create an amazing pyramid of responsibilities for ourselves. It is similar to the obligations of caring for a child. In some ways caring for a pet is even more difficult, since children grow up, become independent and outlive us. Pets do not. They are bound to us for all of their lives. When they die, these responsibilities we created live on in many ways.

CARE PROVIDERS

Sensitive people can be compulsive care givers. In taking on the responsibility for a pet, we accept a burden of total obligation and reliability. This includes caring for every possible aspect of the pet's life; health, happiness and well-being. We volunteer for a duty that quickly becomes a passion and an act of love. As our pets become more and more endeared to us this responsibility becomes a way of life to us. Thus, our attachments to our pets can become lifelong bonds. We care and provide for them as we would for dependent children and a part of ourselves.

We are totally and singly responsible for the pet's nutrition, medical care, toys, playmates, status and quality of life—as well as anything else that may be of concern.

We are unable, however, to be perfect in protecting our pets from all possible dangers. Accidents and illnesses will happen. In a sense, we assume godlike roles to our pets. They look to us to provide and care for everything, and we make possible nearly everything that they experience. But despite our desire to arrange and care, we can't control the universe. When bad things happen, the pet owner can fall victim to what feels like failed responsibility, with all its invented reactions of guilt. Our wisdom lies rooted, somehow, in our human frailty. But our duty is not measured solely by our action or inaction. It is defined by a complexity of circumstances that can be truly beyond our control or comprehension.

Since we must provide everything for the pet, we assume a powerful responsibility that should not be taken casually. We must not miss a feeding; the water dish has to be checked regularly; visual checkups on the pet's appearance and health must be made constantly, and the list goes on. The practice of this total care constantly strengthens our bond with our pets. We become more and more responsible, attentive and loving. This interchange can subtlely become a relief from daily pressures, releasing us into a private, insular world of mutual love and pleasure from the pet. But that, of course, can have its bad sides as well as its good ones.

MUTUAL BONDING

This mutual bonding becomes a wonderful exchange of need and fulfillment between owner and pet. We place our dear animal friends into a unique relationship that may be witness to a more intensely personal side of us than we share with any human. Because of a pet's total dependency on us we take on unrealistic roles of total responsibility. When death claims the pet, we ultimately must come up short.

14

Monument to a gallant soldier. *Photo by George Wirt, © Bide-A-Wee 1992*

Memorial to a beloved ferret.

Courtesy, Abbey Glen Pet Memorial Park

In an ironic psychological turnabout we become dependent on our pets as well. We rely on their needing us. This becomes a strong foundation for each pet owner's sense of security.

There is no place for death in our loving scheme of things. In our society the discussion or consideration of death has been taboo. We know next to nothing about it, and any associations regarding death are very upsetting at best. It scares and mystifies us. Therefore, we discreetly avoid its examination or even reference whenever we can. When the pet eventually dies, as all must, the shock easily can be distorted into a subconscious sense of intense personal failure. As ready as we are intellectually, we are never prepared emotionally. We all need all the help we can get.

Very often even our closest friends and family sometimes can't grasp the depth and extent of our bereavement. We sometimes make this sense of intense responsibility extremely private and secluded from the rest of the world. Others close to us can seem to fail us in our time of need as well, because of their lack of understanding or acceptance of our self-made roles. We owe it to them, as well as ourselves, not to be hair-triggered, and to try to maintain some degree of control during those difficult times.

As suggested earlier, when a beloved pet dies we lose a very close member of our immediate family. We lose a treasured extension of ourselves. But our responsibility is not yet finished. We still have another one as well. That is, that we must live on without the pet. That obligation is our own, one that we have to ourselves in our grief.

We must endure this loss. During the most profound moments of bereavement we can't think in these terms. However, we must still prepare ourselves for it, either in advance or in healthy hindsight.

Aside from mortuary care and expense, our obligation still lives on, demanding that we make our pet's memory a positive, treasured part of ourselves. If we do not treat ourselves with self-respect during the grief of mourning, we diminish our love for the pet as well.

We should not deny the pet's living memory a chance to enrich and improve our lives. We are still obliged this much, at least, in living memoriam. Our lives must go on, enriched by the wonderful experience of having shared so much together.

Some relationships with pets can become pathological when the pet owner assumes a distorted sense of responsibility vastly disproportionate to the reality of the pet's needs. Although many pets are treated as surrogate children, this *can* be a healthy expression. There is concern and possible danger only if owners overlook basic needs for themselves or the pet. We have seen many cases where pets are dressed up like babies, given dolls or infant toys, and even moved about in a small baby carriage. But there is no harm here, even though the behavior may seem bizarre and it denies the true nature of the pet. There is always some possibility, however, that the pet is being abused by not being able to live as an animal. In this instance, we must be concerned with a pet owner who may be losing a grip on reality.

PETS AND SENIORS

Single senior citizens as pet owners tend to be extremely affectionate, even doting on the animal. A pet shares the senior's loneliness and the changes taking place in his or her ability to do things. Whatever losses the older person may have suffered during a lifetime become shared experiences. A person's health and mobility may have deteriorated, but pets love and depend on their owners as much as before. As hearing, sight and general tone diminish, so may one's motivation to savor life. There are fewer visitors, if any, but that becomes alright, if the senior citizen has the ever-present security of one or more pets as loving companions.

Who can appreciate the countless hours older pet owners must have had, talking their hearts out to a pet? This pet shares everything, and becomes a very dear and necessary part of the senior's life. Eventually, when the pet as well shows signs of aging or health deterioration, the owner's dependency is increased. This owner now must become even more of a provider and caretaker. To a benefit, this makes a person feel even more vital and needed.

17

The mutual interchange of need and care becomes very enriching.

Then death comes to the pet, as it must. The shock feels like abandonment. It seems as if nobody really cares, even God. This can usually lead to depression and deterioration in the older person, unless there is some other loving and stabilizing influence in that person's life, other than the pet.

But the senior citizens have one advantage with more advanced age. That is the wisdom that comes with experience over the years. They have seen friends and family die, and have learned to become more philosophical than in their younger years. Although mourning is none the less intense for beloved pets, it is usually more rapid, with a stronger and more positive early resolution. Of course, there are exceptions to this.

CASE HISTORY

A married woman in her early fifties had a problem that illustrates this dependence on a pet. After her children grew up and left home, she adopted an adorable puppy from the local animal shelter. She and her husband were well-off financially, and she didn't have to work. Her husband thought her attention to the pet was cute, but didn't she have other more important things to do now that she was free?

She became very involved with training the puppy, and talked to the dog as if it were a baby. Her need to be a nurturer again was a very powerful influence. She adored the pet, lavishing so much attention on it that the pup eventually became very spoiled. This made the husband even more upset. Her relationship with their grown children was never a strong one, and they rarely ever visited

The dog developed the practice of chasing cars that drove on the isolated street in front of their home. After three years, the dog was hit by a car and severely injured, with the spine and ribs crushed. The veterinarian had to ask the woman's husband to insist that she allow euthanasia immediately. Although the dog was in intense pain, she could not find the strength to do anything but weep in near hysterics. The husband finally gave permission, and the pet was euthanized.

Then the woman withdrew into a severe depression, hating her husband for what he and the veterinarian did. The children came to visit and help, but they were rejected in turn. Although it may have been highly irrational, she felt that her responsibility to the pet was usurped, and that everybody was insensitive to her plight or unwilling to understand.

The real problems, however, were not with the dog. This prolonged incident was only the trigger mechanism that released long-repressed and powerful psychological mechanisms that never had been addressed. After nearly a year of psychotherapy, she was able to reestablish her relationships with her husband and children.

SURROGATE FRIEND

CASE HISTORY

Another case involved a mother who mostly ignored her only child, a daughter. The child had an unloving relationship with the stepfather, who married her mother only a year before. When the girl was six, the mother bought her a dog to preoccupy her. Eventually the dog became the child's whole world, both reality and fantasy. The dog was her best friend, and was with her everywhere, except school. Gradually, the child retreated from other people, into a safe fantasy world. Her dog substituted for friends, siblings and parents as well. Her school grades then began to deteriorate. She behaved badly in school, and did not associate well with her peers.

Then the mother divorced again. After the remarriage, she remained unconcerned and uninvolved with the child's problems, and was attentive only with how things looked on the surface. "Appearances" were more important than reality.

The child's whole world revolved around her pet. She learned to feed and care for the dog, to the mother's relief. At this tender age she had assumed complete responsibility for the pet. In three years the dog developed heartworm and died, and the girl became totally devastated. At age ten she was racked with pain and guilt, and was sure that she should have known how to prevent the death. The case was brought to my attention by a neighbor. Because of the mother's obsession with appearances, she allowed the child to start psychotherapy. Fortunately, her prognosis is good.

This child's problems were deeply rooted in insecurity. The single-parent environment, complicated by a selfish mother, gave the young girl a weak emotional foundation to begin with. The death of the obsessively loved pet was the final blow. As in much less dramatic situations, this bereavement was blown out of proportion by prior existing psychological factors.

Stages of
Bereavement

A Prayer

for

Animals

Hear our humble prayer, O God,
For our friends the animals,
especially for animals who are suffering;
for any that are hunted or lost
or deserted or frightened or hungry;
for all that must be put to death.
We entreat for them all Thy mercy and pity,
and for those who deal with them we ask
a heart of compassion
and gentle hands and kindly words.
Make us, ourselves, to be true friends to animals,
and so to share the blessings of the merciful.

—ALBERT SCHWEITZER

3

The Grieving Process

"Your joy is your sorrow unmasked."
—Kahlil Gibran

"**H**OW LONG must I suffer like this?" wonder those who first endure the grief and upset of bereavement. This is a special time when we need all the help we can get. Generally it may last from several days to several weeks. But there are still some pet owners who feel it is not really socially acceptable to mourn for a pet, as we would for a human. This causes enormous internal conflict and disturbance for them, because they seem to need approval and support to grieve for an animal.

In a very real sense the onset of this bereavement may be regarded as an extreme case of separation anxiety. The well-established patterns of our lives are abruptly terminated by the death of a beloved pet. Suddenly, we are left alone and in a state of shock. The problems that arise can seem overwhelming.

Understanding the psychological responses and phases of grief and mourning that other people have gone through can help us when we are going through this process ourselves. This knowledge can be used as general predictors and means to help the grief-stricken mourner get through the worst of it and understand what is happening.

CULTURAL INFLUENCES

Many people have a culturally influenced fear of grieving, and are frightened at being so controlled by death. Because of this fear, they harm themselves emotionally when they refuse to allow their real feelings to emerge. But these responses, however suppressed, are real and need to be released in order that the person may heal.

Often, a second experience with death is surprisingly more painful than expected. Usually that happens because it stirs up repressed and unresolved feelings that need to be dealt with and released.

The period of mourning and bereavement usually is defined by specific, particularly intense, psychological reactions. Most mental health practitioners work on the precept that the overall pattern of behavior during this time expresses itself in gradual phases or stages. This reaction period is seen as an evolving process in development and healing.

Talking about your loss begins your recovery. Pour out your thoughts and feelings. Share them with people of compassion. It is a loving and necessary beginning of your passage through bereavement.

Although these stages usually are transitional phases of bereavement, they can appear simultaneously or in different orders as well. The terms *stages* and *phases* can be misleading if this is not explained, because they can imply that each will appear in due course and then disappear, as if resolved.

Slightly differing names and order of appearance have been suggested by various writers. For our purposes here, we will build a consolidated outline around six general stages, which are examined in sequence, in the next six chapters:

Shock and Disbelief	Chapter 4
Anger, Alienation and Distancing	Chapter 5
Denial	Chapter 6
Guilt	Chapter 7

Some people prefer naming grief as another stage. This classi-
fication is not listed here, because it is believed that the term is too
general. The entire list presented above encompasses grief in each
and all of the stages. Grieving is so personal that it can't be clearly
defined. Each of us has unique reactions and responses to death.

Grief is not an expression of extreme behavior. Nor is it an
indication of a neurosis or disorder. It is a natural response to
sudden, overwhelming loss, and runs a normal course within wide
margins. It is considered normal as long as grievers are not in any
danger of harming themselves or anyone else. Tender loving care
(TLC) and supportiveness are what they need most while living
through this heartache.

GRIEF IN ALL ITS VARIETIES

Because of the very many variables of personality and the
conditions that trigger them, it is not possible to predict the full
nature and scope of these responses. We have to deal with each of
these painful stages when and how it develops. There are many
factors that can affect us in dealing with our bereavement. These
variables include: past experience with grief and/or death; individual personality differences and histories; degree and quality of
social supportiveness; spiritual, religious, ethnic and cultural influ-
ences; age and gender, and the special nature of the lost
relationship.

CASE HISTORY

One of my patients was a widow whose dog died four
years before she came to me. When the woman's husband died a few years earlier, she was shaken, but seemed

A tribute to one who will live on in memory.   *Courtesy, Hartsdale Canine Cemetery, Inc.*

In memory of a cherished bunny.   *Courtesy, Abbey Glen Pet Memorial Park*

to stand up well to the shock. The mourning period was brief and well handled. It was very important to keep up appearances for the neighbors.

She tried very hard to put on a brave face. All her attention and love now were focused on her dog, who reveled in this. As the years went on the woman grew increasingly dependent on what the dog represented to her. It was made over into a combination of surrogate roles, from child, through best friend, to husband.

When the dog died a few years later, she was overwhelmed by inconsolable grief, and had to be hospitalized for a few days. After an intense period of mourning, which was never resolved, she tried to go about a normal way of life, but couldn't without the dog. She would not get another pet and as a result, her life became entirely devoted to the remembrance of her deceased dog. Her apartment was turned into a near shrine, with pictures draped in black, and the dog's toys and other memorabilia on prominent display. The pet's ashes and urn occupied the central focus of the apartment.

The woman continued this way for a few more years, in perpetual mourning and grief. After analysis, it turned out that much of this abnormal behavior was in response to a deep sense of guilt at not having grieved for her husband as much as she felt she was "supposed to." She was afraid of letting her feelings go. Thus, she could never complete the mourning process for her husband or for the dog.

Her unresolved grief continued until she could be shown that she was not guilty or bad, just very misguided in her previous perceptions. There is a happy ending to this story, since she now is leading a normal life after wasting so many precious years.

Grief can be distorted by symbolic values as well. The pet may represent an important person or an event. The pet might have been treasured by a beloved deceased spouse. Or it could have been the only thing worthwhile salvaged from a bad marriage. Whatever the abstraction, the pet really is made into a functioning symbol of something very important. When the animal dies, this false sense of security dies with it. A blueprint for disaster has been created and is just waiting to be used.

ALLOWING FRIENDS TO MOURN

Generally, it is unwise to intervene in anyone's process of mourning. Offering impressive psychological terminology and explanations may tend to scare the already upset mourners, when they are least in a position to see things as they really are. They may be pressed into feeling that they are "losing it," although this intense behavior may be a normal expression for some individuals at the time.

Too many well-intentioned persons enjoy playing the psychologist. They can cause unintentional harm, making bereavers feel apologetic, defensive or even defective. Any of these can cause the suppression of normal grief responses. That will harm the process that must painfully be allowed to work itself through to reach resolution.

Some surivors of great personal tragedy tend to be stoic in their behavior, especially when it comes to death. As mentioned, these people also may be inclined to suppress rather than hide their feelings and will not willingly resolve their grief through mourning. And there are others who express their repressed sense of guilt as self-punishment and bereavement. Their needs and grief, as well, are not correctly focused and are in need of objective counseling.

A beloved pet becomes part of a human companion. When the pet dies, it becomes the end of an era in that person's life. This death shockingly marks the close of one stage and the beginning of the next.

But each next stage is based on the strengths of the last.

Certainly, the living memory of the pet remains with us as we grow and live on. Each time a beloved pet dies it is like a painful metamorphosis in the life of the owner. Each successive stage allows the mourner to become wiser with age, better and more seasoned with treasured memories and experiences.

It must be mentioned here that there will always be some future emotional aftershocks, long past the period of bereavement. However well adjusted we may be, our loving memories are still there within us. They just are not as obvious as before. It is a normal psychological response to reexperience some of the grief we lived through earlier. Fortunately, this is not as painful or debilitating as before.

An epitaph for a beautiful young lion.   *Courtesy, Hartsdale Canine Cemetery, Inc.*

4

Shock and Disbelief

"O aching time! O moments big as years!"
—John Keats

SHOCK AND DISBELIEF, in various degrees, are the first likely responses to the death of a beloved pet. This early stage may last from a few hours to even a few days. During this time we suffer from a loss of a sense of awareness and proportion in dealing with things. Especially when first experiencing this emotional overload, we usually can't even begin to grip the reality of the situation. The mind is stunned by powerful psychological reactions that can completely overwhelm what feeble strengths we may have at the time. We respond at this stage with a physical or mental numbness that could feel overwhelming. Basic experiences and information related to the death can be "blocked out" and not remembered, just as if they never happened or were not provided.

Counselors trained in human bereavement are familiar with situations in which the question "Is he or she really dead?" is repeated, over and over, despite very specific information or proof. Disbelief is a powerful temporary defense. There is a more familiar situation demonstrating disbelief though. We are all familiar with the expression beginning with "I can't believe . . ." At least in this application the speaker is able to accept the reality, although it seems terrible or even fantastic.

DEFENSES OF THE MIND

In extreme instances the mind can respond to a shock by becoming completely oblivious to the situation. It can refuse to accept any input that supports the shocking news. It is as if a person were hypnotized and instructed to totally ignore certain specific stimuli.

This response of numbness is the mind's way of protecting itself from having to handle too much too soon after the initial shock and sudden impact with death. It is nature's last defense, shielding us from violence that can be done to the mind by unbearable stimuli.

There is a similarity between extreme examples of shock and disbelief and some forms of amnesia. The mind has fantastic defenses. In some cases of child abuse, for example, the child's memories of the offense are completely blocked out. Only rarely does the offense become recalled, and that only after very many years have gone by. The child could be middle-aged or older before even beginning to have any recollection of what really happened.

The mind also plays similar tricks on people suffering from multiple personalities. Because they can't handle stress, nearly any sudden shock or strain will shift them into an invented personality that can deal with such a situation. In staggering under the initial shock, the mind is buying time to be able to live with a situation that is unbearable.

SHOCK AND GRIEF

Shock is sometimes referred to as the onset of a post-traumatic stress syndrome, such as strong bereavement. When the initial reactions of shock and disbelief wear off, an overwhelming flood of other strong emotional responses will follow. This flood of

32

emotion is full of distortions and misperceptions at first. Time will help with the healing, and we must be patient with ourselves, despite how difficult that may seem to be at the moment. Normally, these strange and unpleasant reactions will run their course and fade as part of the mourning process.

But we are dealing with the sudden onset of human tragedy. There is really no way to prepare defenses against shock and disbelief. Powerful emotions, intense reactions and feelings, a sense of violation and utter helplessness and distress can prevail for a while.

We tend not to heal at this time as quickly as we would from other adversities because we may be going through an abrupt separation anxiety. In this particular situation normal daily patterns of living are broken, and we have no other routines that can carry us through. Sometimes the structure of going to work or being seriously involved in some activity will provide the necessary means to keep us going while our inner resources have a chance to rebuild themselves.

There will be times, in the depths of our misery during bereavement, when we will suffer grievously indeed. Because of this extreme response it is not uncommon for people in bereavement to wonder about their sanity. Yet we must realize that there is a difference between this normal, temporary agony and one that may not ease up within a reasonable period of time.

ACUTE GRIEF

Acute grief, also referred to as exaggerated grief, is not an expression of any normal mourning process. This kind of over-reaction is somewhat easy to identify. Some of its many possible symptoms are intensified irritability and sleeplessness, or even their opposites—extreme withdrawal and fatigue. Other indications may be excessive anger, antisocial behavior or persistent nightmares. Sometimes one experiences near-hallucinations such as hearing or seeing glimpses of the deceased pet.

Too often an abnormal response to this post-traumatic stress syndrome is overlooked as something that eventually will go away.

Unfortunately, it does seem to disappear, but it does not really go away. It becomes repressed, where it will fester possibly for the rest of this person's life. There must be a release. Professional help is definitely needed here.

The best generalization that can be made about acute or exaggerated grief is that it is suffered by persons who are least able to cope with it and probably already emotionally injured and suffering from other major stresses in their lives. The weight of bereavement can become the straw that breaks the camel's back.

In bereavement, a normal amount of shock and disbelief are reasonable responses, and should not prove too distressing in their own right. These fade and pass fairly quickly. We all experience this to some degree.

Usually this response is an accurate measure of the emotional intensity that will be expressed in the bereavement stages that are yet to follow.

CASE HISTORY

A single woman in her early thirties went on a month's vacation to Europe. She left her dog with a reputable and expensive boarding kennel. When she returned, she was informed that her dog died of sudden heart failure about a week after her departure. Since there was no way of contacting her, the body was cremated and the ashes kept for her return.

She grew furious at the news, and refused to accept it as the truth. She was certain that there must be some kind of terrible conspiracy and her dog surely must be alive somewhere. Talks with the veterinarians who tried to save the dog, and the managers of the kennel and the crematorium, only intensified her anger and disbelief. She tried, in vain, to call in the police. Then she tried to retain a lawyer, who attempted to advise her about her denial of what had to be reality. This only served to further distress her to the point where she could not even go back to work until she received what she deemed to be satisfaction.

A close friend talked her into coming to therapy for just an initial meeting. Fortunately, we were able to strike a rapport with each other, and follow-up sessions established that she felt totally responsible and guilty for having set up the selfish conditions of her absence during this critical time.

We discussed shock and denial, and the truth began to seep in. She quickly lapsed into a deep depression, during which it became necessary for a psychopharmacologist to prescribe specific drug therapy to be used in conjunction with her psychotherapy sessions.

Fortunately, she was able to return to work in about two weeks, and slowly recovered afterward. Other stresses in her life had been tearing her apart, emotionally, prior to her departure for that well-needed vacation. The death of her beloved dog was the trigger mechanism that set her off into shock and denial. She now sees this, and is working at self-improvement in normal psychotherapy sessions. The prognosis is good.

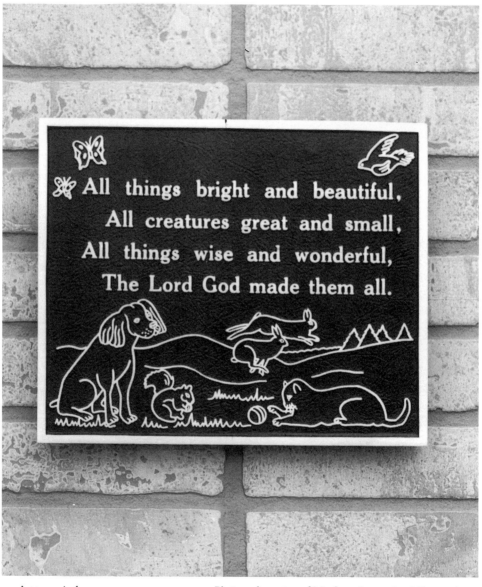

A prayer in bronze.

36

5

Anger, Alienation and Distancing

"Freeze, freeze, thou bitter sky, thou dost not bite as nigh
as benefits forgot. Though thou the waters warp
thy sting is not as sharp as friends remembered not."
—William Shakespeare

THE ANGER STAGE usually is an irrational response to a total sense of frustration and outrage. The outrage results from not being able to understand or have any control. It can take many forms, but is always easily recognizable. Sometimes our pain makes us feel that we have to lash out at someone else, anyone. We are good at creating impassioned excuses in venting the rage within us. In this stage, it is difficult to cope with things and people in general. We displace this anger in all directions, almost at random.

OBJECTS OF ANGER

Anger will appear within us in amazing forms. It can be turned outward just as easily as inward. Self-anger can be acted out as secondary anger, in which there is a displaced, irrational assignment of blame and responsibility onto others.

The absolute nature of death leaves us no bargaining chips. We are totally helpless. This is in stark contrast to the freedom we had in making all decisions before the pet's life was snatched away from us. We now feel helpless and useless, and this is unbearably frustrating. We need to feel anger to vent this sense of sudden checkmate. However, most of us have trouble expressing anger because we are not effective in using it. When we are suddenly immersed in the passions of bereavement, this difficulty becomes many times greater.

Any remotely involved person or authority can be made into a scapegoat. Because of the veterinarian's dominant role in the pet's life and death, the doctor, the hospital and the staff are usually the most assailable, and the first to be blamed. They may be simon-pure, and completely without guilt, but in our passion at the moment we must blame someone or something.

When our pets' lives are "taken," we lose our perspective of right and wrong for the time being. People or situations that can be considered blamable will be condemned, however irrational this may seem at another time. Frustration and rage, multiplied by a violent sense of loss, can distort our sense of proportion. Tiny incidents that normally would be overlooked can be blown up into exaggeration and misconstruction in our passionate need to assign blame at this stage of the mourning process.

It is a normal human trait to turn our anger inward, blaming ourselves for all kinds of imagined weaknesses and faults, in frustration at not being able to prevent the death. Being forewarned, though, can sometimes take the keen edge off this response. It is a loss of the control that we had and took entirely for granted. We even might feel anger at our own survival after the pet's death. That frequently leads to depression, and needs tender loving care rather than rebuttal. But anger is not apt to produce a sympathetic response. It becomes an irrational exercise in self-defeatism.

At this time of bereavement we are very vulnerable. We easily can become overwhelmed by the emotional over the rational. In this state we lose some perspective in our involvement, creating irrational responses to some things. At another time we would not be nearly as upset by what now can possibly set us off into great anger or even rage.

HEALTHY RELEASES

For your own sake, you must eventually understand and control your anger. How long can you sustain and justify this emotional drain on yourself, when it is not really clear what or who is at fault? Withheld anger can become a potent force in self-destructiveness.

Get it out now, and become able to let it go. This is an intensely personal, subjective response. It is also very difficult, and requires you to be honest with yourself. You and your pain deserve better treatment than keeping it submerged. First, we must try to make it more objective. This method is very functional, and should take a few days at least. Do not try to do it all in one sitting.

Make a list headed ANGER.
1. Number each response individually.
2. Skip a line before writing the next one.
3. Write the names of people you are angry at.
4. Make a list of the names of those you feel have upset you, in any way, in your bereavement.
5. After you have finished the list, go back and fill in the reasons for each person's "guilt."
6. Omit your own name.

Then, make a second list with the names of institutions, situations or anything else you feel is answerable in causing you unnecessary pain in your bereavement. Then put the list away for a few days before reading it again. That short span of time can give you greater objectivity.

There is no question that you hurt, and that your terrible loss might have been more clearly understood by people who should know better. Yes, there are always some few insensitive ones who upset you with their callousness or stupid comments about your bereavement. Yet, was there something valid in their lives that prevented them from understanding their own inability to cope with the death you now face? Are they, in effect, acting out their own problems? And are you now, by getting so involved and angry, attempting to make them *your* problems, as well?

Are you really looking for a "peg" to hang your anger on? When will you be willing (or ready) to try to forgive? Was the veterinarian really to blame, or is that part of your emotional upset at having to blame someone or some thing? Sometimes, when we hurt most, we want to strike out at others who matter and failed to help us when we needed it most. A secret cry for love and understanding can turn into a confused sense of "justifiable rage" and "righteous indignation."

Role Play

"Role practice" your anger, acting it out with your analyst if you have one or a close friend. If you are fortunate enough to have some kind of support group, try this with them.

Ask someone else to take your part, understanding how much and why you are hurt by each of the people represented on the list you just made. One at a time, you act out the part of each person on your list, and discuss this with the others present to your complete satisfaction. Consider what possible valid excuses the people on the list might have to offer.

Listen to what the others say. Be fair. There is a lot to be learned about yourself and your anger from this kind of objectivity. It will help you ease your pain.

Might there be some legitimate reason for their not being able to meet your needs at this time? Could it be that death secretly scares them, and they can't handle your situation? Maybe there is something else just as terrible in their lives that you are not aware of. Is it possible that your frustration, pain and disappointment are not letting you accept their problems and human frailty? Perhaps your grief and shock are making you lose perspectives of

40

things for the time being. We can become very narrow-minded and selfish during bereavement.

Is it possible that you are revealing some disproportionate or unrelated responses to your pet's death? What is your real anger about? Could this anger really be at yourself? Maybe it's your own rotten luck, or just hard times. Maybe you blame the establishment, or parents, or a spouse. There are so many people and situations that can affect and upset our lives. Respond candidly and as frankly as you can to this self-examination.

Are you overreacting? That is a probable sign that something else is unconsciously troubling you. When this happens it is easy to make mistaken identification of problems or responses. It is nearly impossible to think clearly and without distortion when anger is present.

REACTING TO THOSE AROUND YOU

Friends, family, colleagues, religion. Where do they come in? Were there any truly adequate attempts by them to help you? Were your expectations of them realistic, knowing them as you do? Or were you really hoping more than expecting? Were they able to share your privacy? Or perhaps you felt they invaded it? Maybe you didn't want to let them touch your secret vulnerability and grief. Are you really able to explain and share your pain? If not, don't blame others for not crossing the unexplained barrier you set up.

Rash actions are easily justified at the moment, but are almost always regretted. Sometimes they cannot be erased later, to our enormous sorrow. In our passion we all too easily can lose perspective of what is good or bad for ourselves. What is the point in being self-destructive when we are really trying to help ourselves? A moment's outburst, however good it feels at that instant, is not worth it.

It is easy to be caught off-balance by those who seem rash and judgmental about our grief. Who among us has not heard the comment that one shouldn't be so upset, because "it was only a pet"? Or that your problem would be over if you just got yourself another one right away? What do they really know about you and your dear pet's death? How could they be so insensitive?

But they are trying to make what they think is a legitimate point from their limited perspective. Does that make them bad? They just can't seem to accept bereavement for a pet, and thus come up very short of our needs and expectations at this terrible time. It hurts even more when our emotional reserve of strength is low.

Our normal defense mechanism is to become angry, perhaps even enough to justify alienation for the time being, feeling as though we never want to see or have anything to do with that person again. When we are irrational or petulant we tend to take dramatic steps that are most often regretted later. But that may be too late.

At a vulnerable time like this we are off-balance, and tend to seek an outlet for all our powerful emotions. It becomes easy to justify an excuse to vilify someone who hurts us now. But we must not go on burning our bridges behind us. Some of the relationships that seem strained at this upsetting time have real value and positive significance in our lives. The immediate response to allow ourselves to be hurt by them is self-defeating. Showing our anger by punishing them with permanent alienation, or even temporarily distancing ourselves from them, may not serve our real purposes.

These people may see pets as possessions, childish playthings and nearly frivolous wastes of time and expense. They probably are very upset and threatened by the hidden meanings of death, which they refuse to confront. They become agitated and short with us for lavishing all our sensitivity on a pet's death, when it is too frightening for them to contemplate any death at all. This probably is somewhat intimidating to them and their weak grasp of the subject. Their defensive behavior can seem rude, belittling or even hostile. How did you respond to this kind of disappointment? It is too easy to be impatient or overreact when overwrought with powerful emotions.

Some people who are close to us may not offer any response

at all to our bereavement. Silence or an absence of a meaningful statement can be too easily mistaken as a critical comment. Almost always, this kind of nonresponse is made because these persons do not know how to respond. Death is a frightening thing. They may well be unable to discuss the subject without feeling greatly threatened. If you love or respect them, don't push, despite your own breaking heart and need for support. They are human, too.

Basic Responses

There are three basic responses you can make to a perceived assault on your grief. The first is to strike back bitterly. The second is to be caught so far off guard that you don't know what to say. Your confused or embarrassed response can probably give the impression that you are not really contradicting or disagreeing. Sometimes a person in authority, such as a boss or supervisor, may have you at this disadvantage if you are not ready for this.

The third and most effective response is to *be prepared, in advance.* You can look such an insensitive person right in the eye and say, "You don't have a pet such as mine, and can't possibly understand what kind of love and understanding there was for me. How can you judge my grief? Please be more tolerant when such deep, personal feelings are involved!"

These are nonthreatening expressions responding to the challenge of the situation. Such responses can maintain the respect you might otherwise lose. And they may keep you in control of the situation. Also, this kind of nonthreatening response might quite possibly elicit an insight which that person could not have reached otherwise. It might help to save a valuable relationship. It might also prevent additional unnecessary suffering for yourself.

Sometimes we are so angry at ourselves that we create social situations that are intolerable to others. Such tendencies indicate a kind of inadequacy, which produces a need to be punished. Overreactions and inappropriate anger are means to getting just what we are unconsciously asking for. This type of neurotic response in not uncommon. But it is nearly always self-destructive to some degree.

It can be difficult to remain cool and unreactive to the perceived hurts and insensitivities all around us at this time. But it is encouraging to know that this emotional turmoil is a stage that will pass if we let out our feelings and express them to caring and sympathetic listeners.

By suppressing these powerful emotions, however irrational they may be, we delay our healing and the ability to resolve our lives with the reality that now exists without the beloved pet. Since death knows no bargaining, we must come to terms with ourselves.

Anger is a highly personalized, emotional response to a perceived offense or violation. It has many legitimate uses as well as abuses. But what valid purpose can anger serve in memorializing a beloved life that has been snatched away? Can we be angry at death or the reality of things? Can we be angry at ourselves for not being able to defeat death? Fortunately, this is only a stage, and will pass if we permit it and give it time to do so.

6

Denial

"Parting is all we know of heaven and all we need of hell."
—Emily Dickinson

DENIAL is one of the earliest stages of mourning. It is easily confused, at first, with disbelief, which accompanies the shock of first learning about the death (see Chapter 4). Actually, denial is something of a modification of disbelief. There are some psychologists who tend to lump these two terms together as minor variations of the same response.

But all this fancy hairsplitting is of no value at all to the deeply bereaved individual who is full of pain. For our purposes here we will consider that in the stage of disbelief, being part of the initial shock, we still have not yet had time to accept the reality. We flat out refuse to believe, as the word indicates. Denial usually develops later, and in this stage we partially acknowledge that the death has taken place, but we are looking for ways to refute it.

We are strongly tempted to deny reality, having become overwhelmed by the terribly upsetting finality of death. There is a natural tendency to still hope that somehow it was a bad dream or some kind of terrible hallucination. We very much want to believe that our pet is not really dead. Passionately, we hope it might all be good again. This sweet fantasy removes us a little from the pain we are going through. But gradually, the grim reality sets back in. The life of the pet is over, gone, ended! The pain is with us now. Denial is usually a brief stage and fortunately it is over quickly.

In our euphemistic society we are trained to believe that "wishing might make it so." The fairy tales and other related types of stories we knew as a child were full of plots in which the good are given a second chance to escape from death or harm. We want to believe that if we all clap our hands at that right moment, Tinkerbell will live again. Maybe, just maybe, concerning our beloved pets, we believe if we wish or pray strongly enough . . .

The innocent child within each of us naturally craves a happy ending. Learning about death is so studiously avoided that we are ever unprepared for its grim reality when it comes. And it does come to all living things, despite our fancies and fantasies and most fervent prayers.

FANTASY AND OTHER MECHANISMS

Initial denial is an unconscious psychological mechanism to delay a reality that is overwhelming. It serves as a protective means to put us in some sort of painless limbo for a while. Usually, denial in bereavement lasts only a short while. Other realities quickly close in, forcing us back to the fact of the death and our private loss. As painful as it is, we are going through the necessary developmental stages of the mourning-healing process It becomes a transitional state in our personal metamorphosis.

In understanding only some of the fantastic capabilities of the human mind, it is not really surprising to learn that there are two types of denial we can experience.

Delayed denial is more given to contemplation than initial denial. It comes later, usually after the body of the pet has been provided for, and all the other immediate responsibilities are taken care of. It seems to crop up in us when we are alone, smothering in grief, frustration, rage, and a sense of helplessness. The pet's presence is still very strong and we still unconsciously anticipate a greeting at the door when we come home. The apartment or house seems too empty. It doesn't feel real. There is an upsetting sense, almost as if reality has gone through some sort of time warp and things will revert to the way they were. Maybe the pet really isn't dead. Maybe if we try to make some bargain with God the pet will come back again. Therefore, in the denial stage we see the psychological need and function of what is termed *bargaining*. Sometimes this plays a much more impassioned role even before death actually happens, if it is anticipated. But bargaining doesn't ever work. Here it is, now, after the fact. And a *fact* it remains. And all our tears and passion can't wash it out.

Sometimes we need to regress to a fantasy and childlike state of make-believe. As in fairy tales, most kinds of magic are supposed to perform wonderful things. Oh, how we want to believe! For example, if we put out the food dish, maybe, somehow, our pet will come to eat. This is a lovely fantasy up to a point. But it is not real. We have to let go. The death is over and done with, and we are being carried onward in the stream of life and daily responsibilities. The pet has died, time is passing and we must go on.

People who did not personally witness the death more commonly fantasize about the pet still being alive somehow. Pet owners who have to be told about their pet's death while they were away frequently have a more difficult time accepting the immediate reality. The shock of having to be informed about something so intensely personal can aggravate the problem. This appalling end to such a very close relationship is announced by a stranger—a third, unwelcome party to this personal relationship. That feels wrong somehow. It is almost like some kind of desecration of a secret and intimate covenant.

DROPPING DEFENSE MECHANISMS AND ACCEPTING REALITY

Most veterinarians have developed a sensitivity to this situation through experience and common sense. Today, all veterinary

"One Small Furry Friend" bronze plaque. *Photograph courtesy of Matthews International Corporation*

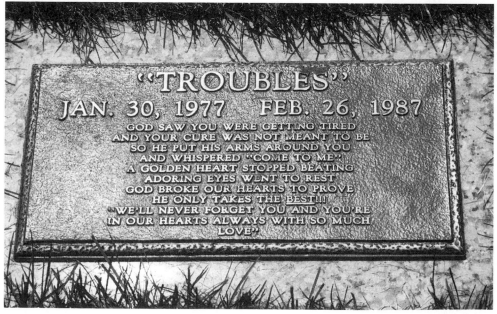

"Come to me."   *Courtesy, Abbey Glen Pet Memorial Park*

colleges and teaching hospitals are finally training their personnel in this. They find that it is important to have pet owners actually see the body if they can. This is to add that final reality to what had been words and abstractions. The newly bereaved pet owner is best served by having some private time, alone, with the body. The first grief should be together if possible.

That can be overwhelming for some people, and they need to maintain some slight distance emotionally. They fear their own responses in particular, as they do death in general. It is a terrible self-confrontation most people don't really know how to handle safely or even comfortably. But because we have been taught by convention to avoid talking or thinking about death, we fear it blindly.

We understand, intellectually, that death comes to all things. But our trained avoidance of this ultimate reality gives us some excuse, up to a point, for denial and bargaining. When faced with death, we actually know a lot more about it than we do about ourselves. And that scares us as well.

Denial is expressed in unlimited ways. There are very many different personal expressions of this normal but temporary psychological reaction. Some expression of denial is actually one of the most common defense mechanisms observed in bereavement. We all feel it, even if slightly or momentarily.

The treatment of extreme cases, however, is to generally accept the denial until the patients are ready to give it up on their own—unless there is psychological risk involved. If they feel pushed, or if the denial is criticized too harshly or suddenly, there is a chance of intensifying other concurrent psychological problems. A defense mechanism is justifiable, even valuable, when it serves as a temporary "Band-Aid" for protection from immediate overwhelming problems. It should not last too long, only a sufficient time to allow reality and natural healing to set in. If it is excessive, then the problem should be addressed by a trained professional.

Defense mechanisms are created by the human mind when it needs to hide from some very painful reality. Acceptance of the full truth in one's bereavement is extremely difficult and full of suffering. It will take some people much longer than others to get through this terrible time. We must be tolerant and patient during this especially difficult transition. The varied forms of denial will modify themselves into other expressions and eventually fade away.

CASE HISTORY

A retired widow in her late fifties was referred because of her acute denial concerning the death of her beloved dog. She had suffered an intense bereavement for her husband, about five years before, and had found much comfort in the dog's loving presence. The relationship between the woman and her eleven-year-old pet had always been close, but now it became very dependent as well. She doted over the dog, to the point that her close friends felt it was becoming a spoiled brat. This became so obvious and obnoxious that she was criticized by nearly everyone. Her response was to escape into a lonely life without company. She rarely saw people any longer, no one other than her adored pet.

Then, as must always eventually happen, the pet died. There was nothing the veterinarian could do to prevent it. The dog was about sixteen years old, and its heart just gave out in its sleep. Although she was fortunate in that her dog died peacefully, the personal tragedy overwhelmed her.

After an elaborate funeral and burial, she decorated her apartment with every possible reminder of her beloved dog. Pictures and toys were prominently displayed, with black and purple crepe everywhere announcing her bereavement. Very few friends and family visited her at first. About three days into her bereavement she started praying fervently for the dog's return to her. Every possible fantasy was utilized, and

50

she lived in the belief that a "simple miracle" would happen, that reality would, somehow, be reversed for her. Everything was put in a state of "hold" until the pet was returned. Nothing could dissuade her from this passion.

Friends and family tried to show her the error of her thinking. This only made the situation worse, and she refused to let them into the apartment any longer. Fortunately, a friend she still listened to was able to persuade her to seek professional help to ease her terrible grief.

We worked on her unresolved bereavement for her husband and her great fear of death. It was important not to stress her irrational feelings of denial though. In time she began to accept the painful reality, and the denial ceased—slowly at first. Most of the unavoidable visual reminders of her pet were removed from the apartment, with only a small shrinelike area remaining. After about two months of psychotherapy she was ready to start her life over again. The prognosis now is excellent.

The unloved are loved.   *Courtesy, Hartsdale Canine Cemetery, Inc.*

In memory of a beloved horse.   *Courtesy, Abbey Glen Pet Memorial Park*

7

Guilt

"All of the animals except man know that the principal business of life is to enjoy it."

—Samuel Butler

GUILT is a psychological construct based on insecurity or a negative self-evaluation. It is a normal response to failing some duty or obligation. It differs from disappointment in that guilt admits to failing to perform at a level well within our levels of competence. It is closely related to the emotion of shame, based on some negative response that could have been prevented.

Interestingly, guilt is not limited to people, although it is a human invention. We can see it when training or scolding our pets for violating what they already understood to be an expected behavior. An animal, however, would not feel guilt on its own. That is an emotional response that we have imposed, with our unending list of rules and regulations. Not surprisingly, in the wild guilt has not been observed.

GUILT AND BEREAVEMENT

But here we are particularly interested in the feelings of guilt and failed obligation that crop up during our intense bereavement

53

for a pet. Whenever we accept the responsibility for a companion animal, we willingly take on a moral presumption of total reliability. This sense of duty concerns every possible aspect of its life, health, happiness and well-being. It becomes a powerful self-obligation that may well suffer from a lack of perspective. Unfortunately, such a driving attitude of obligation can create a vicious cycle that has no provision to ever end. There usually is no place for death in our loving scheme of things. It scares and mystifies us, so we politely avoid thinking about death whenever we can. When death eventually does come, the shock easily can be distorted into an intensified sense of personal inadequacy and guilt. In effect, our emotions tell us we have failed, in some way, to perform as well as we should have. It makes us feel as if we are responsible for letting the pet die.

Total Responsibility

We are totally and singly responsible for the pet's nutrition, medicines, medical care, toys, playmates, sexual status and quality of life. The bonding that results is two-way, with the human becoming emotionally dependent on the pet as well. During the intense emotions of bereavement, we fall victim to our all too human response, creating a powerful sense of guilt. We failed to be in total control. We were unable to be perfect in completely protecting the pet from all possible dangers. This particularly applies to death, whenever that will be. In a sense, we assume godlike roles to our pets, but we are still fallible. That is ever so loving, but we can't control the universe. Whatever wisdom we have lies rooted in our human frailty.

Our responsibility is not solely measured by action or inaction. It is defined by a vast complexity of circumstances that can go beyond our control or comprehension. Despite this reality, we respond with our emotions, as if we, somehow, should have been able to alter or even prevent the contributing factors in the pet's death.

Generally, during the earliest stages of mourning, powerful feelings of anger, grief and guilt can overwhelm us. These easily distort most attempts at objective thinking. Such irrational pain can be the result of dwelling on what we fantasize "might have been." All kinds of "If only . . ." load our minds to bursting. We begin to feel as if we had not been sufficiently responsible. We are human, so we long for what we can't reach. What else could or should have been done? "Why didn't I do something else?" "How did I fail my pet?" Do these sound familiar?

Death has always been a mystery, and despite all our self-driven senses of guilt and responsibility, it will always remain one.

Blame

Since you can't blame death, you blame yourself or others in the midst of your painful coping with grief. It was a loss of control. You had complete responsibility and it was taken from you. But by assigning blame, even to ourselves, we feel we can retain a sense of control that was lost.

Indeed, it never existed. Intellectually this doesn't make much sense, but emotionally it makes all the difference. Maybe you could have done things differently. But isn't this true about everything? This really is an exercise in fantasy that abuses reality as well as ourselves. Its underlying purpose is to give an excuse to blame or punish ourselves in our anguish. It offers a seemingly tangible excuse for death, which otherwise would upset us even more. It is out of our control.

Nobody can really explain to satisfaction why fate sometimes seems so cruel. So we fall victim to blaming ourselves in retrospect. We ponder, now without purpose, about what we may have done or not done possibly to have prevented, postponed or eased this death. Often we digress into useless fantasy that can result in great personal pain and self-abuse.

CASE HISTORY

There was the case of a woman who had her cat declawed after it destroyed furniture and drew blood from her.

This seemed the most sensible thing to do at the time. It made life bearable with an otherwise angry and destructive pet. The owner was a person of great responsibility, and she had a deep affection for the cat despite bad behavior. It was well understood that without this extreme measure she would have had to give the cat up. However, this logic later gave way to irrational feelings, as it so easily can during the grief and confusion of death.

About two years later, the cat died from feline leukemia. The woman shifted this chaotic, bewildering grief into feelings of guilt. Somehow, she now blamed herself for making the little remaining time in her pet's life less than it could have been without her interference. She was now convinced she was guilty of making a bad decision to declaw the cat.

During grief, reality and rationality sometimes get lost. As shown, guilt can be completely unfounded. It may be a neurotic response in reacting to something we perceive as a failure. Way down deep, some individuals even feel that any kind of guilt and pain are part of a deserved self-punishment for who or what we are. A perpetual sense of guilt becomes a way of life for these individuals.

Loss of Control and Afterthought

Death is sensed as a loss of control when you felt that you had complete responsibility. If you can't fully accept the personal blame (and nobody can), then you may need to pass it on. It is easy to assign fault at this time of emotional distraction. Therefore, we create atmospheres in which we tend to develop intensified responses. These usually are very much out of proportion to the realities of the situation. They also may abet the onset of depression.

Guilt also can be a product of afterthought. It is more easily created in the mind of one who is already vulnerable and suffering.

Turn-of-the-century memorial.   *Courtesy, Bide-A-Wee 1992. Photo by George Wirt*

This serves no other real purpose but to hurt the one who invents this guilt.

It is normal to wonder about possible alternatives we may have taken, but to feed a mind-set of self-punishment is a distortion. Mistakes can be made, but that is the way humans operate. Nobody is perfect or exempt, especially in heeding the overwhelming responsibilities we impose on ourselves with our pets.

Guilt is often a warping of afterthought and reflection. Pet bereavement frequently is beset with such dilemmas. These uncertainties often concern euthanasia or impossible thoughts about what we might have done better had we only acted differently. If we only had second sight! But we do not. We are human and imperfect, blessed with love and a sense of the ideal. Each expression of guilt needs to be examined separately to determine the reason it was created.

But death has slammed the door of life in our face before we could grasp its full significance. When we try to comprehend this shock, so many new problems and questions become apparent.

Religion and Guilt

Anger can be directed toward religion,, and that can create feelings of guilt. Attempted explanations of either death or God don't really give the answers needed now, in your grief. You are overwhelmed with feelings that question why such an innocent, good, trusting, loving animal must die. It doesn't make sense.

It is easy to believe that most pets are better than many humans. They are pure love, acceptance and trust. The many evils of humanity did not corrupt the purity of their spirit. Why doesn't organized religion offer help in understanding the souls of animals? Do animals have the promise of some heaven, too? Does that same place include us? Does our love rejoin after death? Why can't anyone understand these things? Where does the bereft heart turn? To whom? To what? In trying to better understand our sense of failed responsibility we need time and supportiveness from others, those who are sensitive to our needs and responses.

But ultimately, we must find that final measure of strength

within ourselves. We lose our perspectives when there is death. We do have the redeeming grace, however. Our pets loved us despite all our frailties. What was the good they sensed in us? It must have been real. It must still be real.

RESPONSIBILITY TO OURSELVES

Responsibility now must be to one's self. Be the wonderful person that your pet saw in you. The constructive grieving, letting go of the pain and preserving of loving memories are your duty now. Think about this.

Your life and energy are being wasted feeling guilt because you wish things had been different. This is misplaced and negative energy. Guilt is a normal, personal, human response to having committed some perceived offense. But we are not guilty for not considering all possibilities—or for not thinking at the right time. Since we are human we also make mistakes. If they are not viciously intended, don't we deserve forgiveness and some compassion as well? Certainly! But it has to come from within one's self.

CASE HISTORY

The problems of another patient can illustrate this. Here we have the case of a young woman in her late thirties who lovingly housed two stray kittens until she could find a home for them. This gave her great pleasure and took about two weeks to accomplish. But her real pet, an older cat, felt jealous during this period.

A few months later this pet suddenly came down with a previously undiagnosed congestive heart problem. Her pet died just three weeks later, despite every possible attempt at medical assistance.

The young woman could not overcome her grief, feeling guilty about not showing "enough love" to her cat when it must have been feeling ill, even though she did not know this. She began to recall how her pet misbehaved and was punished when the kittens were being temporarily housed and cared for. She felt that this surely must have deteriorated her pet's quality of life, somehow contributing to the heart disease and early death. She felt this, but did not really believe it. But she was vulnerable, and a deep sense of personal guilt was being given free rein over her. Fortunately, she sought professional psychological advice, and soon was helped out of this terrible state of mind.

The potential for inventing guilt is vast, and the human mind does some powerful damage to itself at times. Where does one realistically draw the line on responsibility and its fulfillment? Both we and our beloved pets stray a bit from perfection, and this should be realized and accepted. That amazing, loving bond between a human and pet is so special that any transgression is quickly over-looked. It is overwhelmed by our love of being together. But we must punish our pets, at times, just as we do our children. This is the way they sometimes must be shown how to behave. Isn't a well-trained, well-behaved pet a happier one? Surely the training process is necessary, with all its occasional upsets and losses of patience.

But we still are plagued by those nagging, sinking feelings of what we could or should have done "if only . . ." This is so common during the grief and irrationality of bereavement when we are most vulnerable to self-doubt and invented guilt of all kinds.

Responsibility as Keeper and Protector

In our role as keeper of a pet, we have assumed such total responsibility that we are psychologically unprepared for the sudden release of that responsibility without our consent. After a lifetime of self-accountability we still feel responsible, and the

60

feeling does not go away with the pet's death. The patterns we have established over such a long period of time keep us in bondage to them. Since all decisions had been up to us, it is normal to feel that there may have been other things we could have done. This easily develops into a deep, personal sense of guilt that we might have done something *else* to avert this death.

Accidents Do Happen

There may be times when guilty feelings seem justified, when for the most part they are not. These become exaggerated by such thoughts as "it wasn't the pet's time to die yet." But, obviously, it was. Abstract feelings of life crashing, out of control, seem to dominate our thoughts.

When there was no time to say good-bye, we are particularly upset. We even feel cheated by not having had the chance to see the pet die naturally. But when is that ever easy? Even though we know better, we never feel it is time. An emotional conflict with reality can create upsetting feelings of anger. We can become obsessed with pondering how destiny is preventable. In the larger picture, what then, if anything, is fully mutable? How much control do we really have over our fates? Some philosophers claim that everything that happens is natural.

Even carelessness, in all its impossible degrees, should be seen in this light. Leaving the dog outside on a frayed leash or the cat with an open window or poisonous plant leaves are not uncommon happenings. The guilt experiences of most of us are many and more varied than one would normally imagine.

There are accounts of all kinds, such as that of the puppy on an outdoor tether being attacked by a possibly rabid, stronger animal. There was a sweet kitten that was carried off by a hawk in front of the horrified pet's owner. One of the most bizarre of these events happened when a man's dog accompanied him fishing at a pond just outside the man's home in Florida. An alligator seemed to appear out of nowhere. It sneaked up and seized the dog in those terrible jaws, dragging the startled pet into and under the water, while the man shouted and watched helplessly. Another woman discovered, in shock and horror, that she had backed her car over her beloved dog, fatally injuring her pet. All of these awful events resulted in terrible feelings of guilt for the pet owners. Each one felt he or she could have prevented the pet's death by being more diligent. They all believed it was their failed responsibility. They condemned themselves and punished themselves as guilty.

But we can't be on guard all the time, and we are not all-wise as well. Death even can be caused by the normal use of anesthetic during a simple operation. Indeed, there are risks we haven't even thought about. *It is impossible to prevent all accidents.* All we can do is try to improve the odds of survival. We live with danger all the time. A normal street crossing is a potential hazard. One could even be killed by a piece of falling meteorite. Who can say there should have been preventive action?

The concept of an accident involves chance over control at the moment. But the physical violence was a very disturbing factor in these examples of accidental deaths. It exaggerated all of the varied rationales and feelings of responsibility. Sadly, such guilt can't reverse the control that these people didn't even have at the moment of tragedy.

Legitimate Responsibility

There are some legitimate considerations of possibly being partly responsible in those examples cited above. Shock and grief easily distort our facility for rational thinking, at least temporarily. Certainly, one did not wish or subconsciously plan the pet's demise. But even other minor incidents, which have no real bearing on the pet's death, will readily come to mind at these times of anguish as additional justification for guilt.

We are human, and when we suffer deep emotions we tend to depart for a while from the benefits of logic. There are so many bereaved people whose pets were killed in all sorts of accidents, yet these poor guilt-ridden people suffer merciless self-reproaches with every kind of imaginable possibility and variation of "What if . . . ?"

62

Guilt is an invented response to accepting responsibility that we are not able to bear up. We each have such varied and unique complexities of personality that no generalization will ever satisfy all. It is hoped that by examining each example in this perspective, we can more effectively help ourselves in dealing with this problem at this particularly grievous time in our life.

"Sleeping"; at one with nature.   *Courtesy, Hartsdale Canine Cemetery, Inc.*

Memorial to the adored pets of Vern and Irene Castle.
Courtesy, Hartsdale Canine Cemetery, Inc.

8

Depression

"There is no greater sorrow than to recall a time of happiness in misery."

—Dante

DOCTORS SPEAK of diseases in terms of their mortality and morbidity. The mortality of a condition is a reference to its killing ability, whereas the morbidity is measured by its degree of misery and pain. Today, a strong case of the flu has a very low mortality index, but its morbidity is quite high. The same can be said of the depression phase of the mourning process. It is often the most troubling stage we have to go through. Fortunately for many, it can be brief as well as mild.

Intense bereavement normally will produce a whole spectrum of powerful emotions and psychological responses. We feel battered by the loss, anger, outrage and frustration that has weakened us. Our inner strength seems to give out, and things begin to feel overwhelming.

All we seem to care about is the pet's death and our own misery. A sense of numbness and indifference creeps over everything else, and we don't care. We feel overwhelmed and very sad. These are signs of the onset of depression. It is not unusual to go through this phase and there is no shame to it. We all have experienced this, the lowest part of the bereavement period.

THE PHASES OF DEPRESSION

Psychologists classify depression as a syndrome characterized by markedly lowered mood tone, difficulty in thinking and unusual physical fatigue. There may be signs of anxiety, obsessive thinking, appetite loss and difficulty with normal sleep patterns. It is characterized by an overwhelming sense of conscious psychic suffering, dejection and despair. Things do not seem to matter much, and the sufferers feel ambivalent about nearly everything. Generally, they prefer to be alone, to stew in the juices of their misery.

Depression can develop to any degree of intensity, but need not cause alarm unless it seems to pose a danger to the subject. Generally, that would be indicated by the emotional health of the pet owner prior to the tragedy. In this state the mind temporarily shuts out things that can cause it pain. By depressing all our senses we numb our grief, which offers a sometimes necessary escape from its intensity for a while.

FEELINGS OF SUICIDE

Suicidal feelings are much more common than is generally believed. Fortunately, they are most often only in a fantasy state and not attempted. Severe depression poses a more serious potential danger, though. Repeated or strong self-destructive thoughts are not unheard of during bereavement for a pet. This should always be counseled by a qualified practitioner of mental health. There is no shame in it. However, a normal range of depression as a phase of bereavement is usually a relatively minor episode despite the heartache involved. This usually will pass in a few days or so.

Only a tiny percentage of depressed mourners entertain serious considerations about suicide. They almost always have well-defined long histories of emotional upset and disturbance. The grief of bereavement is only their trigger mechanism for these thoughts, not a cause.

It can be said that depression is probably the most normal of all responses to the death of a pet. We become depressed in differing degrees at the loss of anything we hold dear. This includes our habits and patterns of behavior, as well as possessions. Even the owner of a smashed-up car or a damaged boat gets depressed by such an event. Certainly the death of a beloved pet would be a reasonable cause for the onset of some depression.

WITHDRAWAL

During this phase of mourning we generally withdraw from the rest of the world. People and incidents don't affect us as they normally do. In the more severe cases of depression, we become listless, sad, uncaring about anything except the pet we have lost. We can feel weak and empty, and no longer find pleasure in things like food, music, humor or any forms of entertainment. Frequent crying is a common absorption. It is difficult to concentrate on things at this time. We just don't feel good about anything, nor do we want to feel better. We tend to sleep fitfully and more often, trying to avoid feelings as well as the reality that has hurt us. At this stage of bereavement, our sense of self-worth can be at its lowest, and we really don't seem to care much about anything.

Depression dulls even our powerful guilt responses, as well as pangs of conscience and shock. We become quiet, dull, listless, melancholy and ambivalent about things in general. Nothing seems to motivate depressed mourners as they withdraw into themselves.

It seems as if there is nothing left in the world to ever smile at again. We are in a retreating, self-protective state of mind during this stage. Our sorrow for ourselves and our pet acts like a barrier between us and the rest of the world. It can seem as if it takes all of our best energies to just endure. Even gentle, caring friends who want to help may seem to be pushy and invasive to the depressed person. We need to be alone more and cry. It may feel at this time that feelings for the deceased pet are too personal and intense to even try to share with anyone else. We need some time and privacy to recover through our depression.

We can even "lose" ourselves for a while, in total and disproportionate focus on the beloved companion who is now dead. We are distraught because religious and philosophical teachings don't assure us of an afterlife for this pet, and we are unsure whether we will ever meet again after death.

It is depressing because there are no answers when we need them most. We may feel at this time that life has little or no more value. The future seems to have no meaning or importance. This can be a normal response to bereavement trauma.

Feelings of personal responsibility and failure often stimulate guilt and depression. We are most vulnerable now, as we are our own best scapegoats for things temporarily beyond our control. Feelings of guilt can run unchecked for a while, especially during this phase.

A HEALING STAGE

Depressed mourners desperately need tender loving care. How and where can they get it? Only in cases of abnormal depression is the bereaved unable to take even some small action in this direction. Most of us will pass more easily through this seemingly unending but healing stage. It helps greatly to be able to talk out our story to some sympathetic person or persons. Support groups and trained pet bereavement personnel are probably your best help, especially during this, the saddest phase of the mourning process.

Surprisingly, depression as a stage in bereavement does serve a good purpose. It gives us the time to live with and incubate the grim, new reality. We meditate on the pet's death and begin to develop a new emotional strength and perspective that we could not have had before.

When the depression passes, we are much closer than before to the resolution stage of the mourning process. Things are beginning to look upward now. The worst part is over. For the first time since the death it is possible to sense some light at the end of the tunnel.

CASE STUDY

The patient is an attractive, single woman in her late thirties. She was lonely and moderately depressed to begin with. She owned a large male dog that eventually had been accepted as her protector and surrogate "companion." There was strong therapeutic value in this for her, but it was compromised by her becoming somewhat reclusive, giving up on marriage or ever finding a suitable boyfriend. There was a long history of lowered self-esteem and weak ego strength. She had always felt somewhat depressed and alone. Her alcoholic father was deceased, and her elderly mother, with whom she never had a close relationship, lived halfway across the country. Her only sibling, a brother, had been estranged from her for many years.

The dog died quite suddenly and unexpectedly from a respiratory ailment with cardiac complications. She went into shock and deep depression. She felt abandoned, mildly suicidal and completely alone. Her job suffered, and the rest of her time was spent alone at home. She believed that nothing could ever make her smile again. Fortunately, her alert and compassionate veterinarian noted some of these danger signs, and finally persuaded her to come for counseling.

Psychotherapy began by giving her a secure outlet for her grief. After an initial few sessions of sharing her plentiful pain, anger and guilt, we were able to plan some constructive direction in her thinking. Focus was placed on her family and friendly relationships, as a child and young adult, before she moved away. Once we got into serious analysis and therapy of her more formative years she was able to come out of the clinical depression that was only triggered by the dog's death.

In about a month her bereavement was able to progress to a reasonable resolution. Then we went on, in detail, to analyze what factors existed in her life that made her overreact so strongly to her pet's death. After a few months, she started to become fully aware of the symbolism her dog had and her reasons for shyness and low self-esteem.

She is still in long-term therapy, but now leading a much broader and happier social life. She is still a bit defensive, and laughs about her "pet rock" that needs no sustenance or care and can't die. Frequent travel vacations have begun to help give her a new base to improve her ego strength. Her social life is much improved, and growing even healthier. Now her dream is to settle down to raise a small family, with a dog. The prognosis is excellent, as constructive therapy continues.

9

Resolution

"Our deeds still travel with us from afar.
And what we have been makes us what we are."
—George Eliot (Mary Ann Evans)

THERE IS A TIME to have, to hold, and a time to let go. We will know joy just as we must know sorrow. This final phase of one's period of mourning is a time of spiritual inner healing. It is the time for releasing the pain without diminishing the beloved memory. Resolution is the knitting up of open wounds, but there will always be a secret scar. It is the taking of a brave step forward, putting things into new harmony. This is finally the time for letting go. That means allowing the focus of emotion and attention to be shifted, permitting us to continue with our own life's growth. This is when our pain changes from an immobilizing force to one of precious remembrance, hope and self-regeneration.

Our life goes on, but we never let go of the love that still is so cherished. It becomes a fundamental passion within us, never to be lost. What we do with that and how we may choose to "memorialize" it will vary with each individual.

Enduring passage through the mourning process in no way will degrade our intensely personal love for deceased pets. Rather, this is the sometimes difficult part of each mourner's life, when functioning must be resumed. But now each of us is different from before, left without that special pet's physical presence and companionship.

INEVITABILITY

Death is the inevitable and only destination of every life. It is that simple. We so easily accept the concept of birth and living, but we become upset and troubled by thinking about the end of life. Because it is so completely unknown and only guessed at, this subject becomes too disturbing to confront when not absolutely necessary. Most of our experiences with death are rationalized or blocked out. We pretend to ourselves, and try to deny that death is always around the corner *in every life*. We like to make believe that it can be controlled by modern medicine, when it is only postponed at best.

But right now, during the mourning process, we are tossed back and forth by life and death. At first our fate is to be helpless against these forces. Death has come again, and we are ever so unprepared. Even the word *death* provokes general discomfort. As a natural result, many word substitutes and euphemisms have been created. We even think in euphemistic ways, avoiding direct confrontation with the subject. People don't generally discuss death. It is usually extremely uncomfortable even hearing others talk on this topic. Thus, we are always unready and frightened, as well as completely overwhelmed by the grim finality.

CULTURAL ADJUSTMENT

Our culture needs to make an adjustment. Fortunately, it is beginning to show some change. This is accomplished only by cumulative individual acts, however. Death is a natural part of life. Like birth, it is only a marking point of life. All living things must die. We like to feel we have gained such mastery and control over

Dedicated to the memory of the unknown canine soldier.

Courtesy, Hartsdale Canine Cemetery, Inc.

73

life and illness that death is a mistake, an accident, and can be constrained.

It is interesting to note that underdeveloped civilizations accept death much more easily and rationally than we do. That is not because they are less sensitive or intelligent. Simply, they have not yet been fooled into believing that Nature can be controlled so completely. All our powers of civilization cannot revoke death. All the command and dominion we have attained over other things is useless. We cannot pretend that death does not follow naturally.

As enlightened individuals, we would improve ourselves if we changed our attitude that death might go away if ignored. Time and death will catch up with us. It always does, and should not be thought of as something arcane, supernatural or bad. Death, as a natural event, is nothing to be feared.

Mourning for a pet has always been kept very private and secret, as a means of self-protection from unqualified criticism. We have reached a point in our cultural evolution where this humane expression finally is being let out from under wraps. People are beginning to talk more freely about the effect of a pet's death upon them. One's personal vulnerability and the stigma of shame are being reduced or removed. So many others are being made aware of the vast numbers of us who have experienced this grief. We are no longer looked upon as social oddities. There is some encouragement in this realization, when we must no longer feel as restricted in expressing our heartfelt feelings and responses to a pet's death.

DURATION OF MOURNING

There is no easy answer to how long the deep grief of mourning will last. It helps the healing process when we change or modify our daily routines that formerly involved the deceased pet. Often, too many constant physical reminders and associations left about the house become very upsetting. It would be useful to remove or monitor at least some of these, for the time being at least. If we allow ourselves to speak about our loss and grieve freely, the mourning period will be shorter and more constructive. We let some of the pain out this way, which makes room for healing. Indeed, in clinical studies it has been found that some people have never truly completed their mourning needs and process. Therefore, they suffer more than they should, and suffer needlessly for many years—even for the rest of their lives.

DISPLACED GRIEF

Occasionally, some of us are affected by another personal loss that has not been resolved. When a second strongly upsetting death involves us, we may well suffer from displaced or augmented grief. Mourning for a pet this time could be interwoven subconsciously into our unresolved previous mourning, even for a person. Whatever grief is experienced here may well be aggravated by any other prior emotional difficulty, regardless of the origin. Such a situation would do well with professional assistance. Anything that helps people to see the problem with better objectivity is worth investigating.

We must recognize that mourning is a process that must run its course through natural stages of self-repair. If this is disrupted, the healing process will be as well. People who fear to acknowledge or express even the normal grief they feel will impede their own healing process. By sharing our feelings when we can, we improve our own humanity and live on. This is part of the process. It is fundamental to the way we are.

LETTING GO

The entire mourning process is a living-through situation in which we are unconsciously preparing ourselves, step-by-step, to let go of what we hold so dear. The very term *letting go* can be misleading. It does not mean forgetting or the end of loving memories. This letting go comes gradually, with the acceptance of the grim reality and its effects upon us. It is achieved when thoughts of a beloved pet no longer occupy the forefront of one's mind. It permits us to remember and feel all the love, without the shock and grief caused by a pet's death. Yet it is a means of resolution, with which we can pick up our emotional mess and go on with our own living.

THE FINAL STAGE

This final stage of the mourning process is achieved one painful step at a time. We experience it when we begin to sense the pet's loving memories as part of our personal roots. From this we can go on, without guilt or debilitating grief. We identify it when we suddenly become aware that some of the irrational intensity that has governed our grief has passed.

It is often said that time heals all wounds. Superficially, that statement is correct. But it is trite and incomplete. A better statement would explain that what really heals is learning to live with wounds. That requires time to achieve and complete. Time can dull memories; that is not what we seek here.

In time, we never lose that special sense of bereavement for a beloved life. However, we do learn to be less and less overwhelmed by this death. We learn to let go of the shock and pain, but not the countless loving memories and associations. And we go on living.

The process of gradually picking ourselves up to continue with our lives involves a multitude of different considerations. But, somehow, these are accomplished in time. Mostly, they are made at the subconscious levels of awareness and healing. Gradually, as the shock diminishes, we are able to go on.

There are some who even respond as if they have become a different person. Indeed, they have changed. Others may feel a spiritual dedication to the pet's living memory, and redirect their lives accordingly. We move on, with time. We step up on the staircase of experience, ever changing and slightly different as we go. With each step we are more aware, and hopefully wiser. The experience of living with a beloved pet has been an enriching one,

one that benefits us forever. It adds a certain special endearing memory and strength to us, now and in the future.

We become products of our former experiences. After discovering the beauty and wonder of that special loving life, we owe it to that living memory to heal and grow ourselves. We must go on. Certainly, that is what the pet would want for us, if we were to be able to put that pet's feelings into human thought. Consider that.

It is enriching to think that your new life alone, without the deceased pet, can become a living memorial. Each of us can become an example of loving memory for our dear ones who have passed on before us. What we make of our lives now is the ultimate testimony to that love.

MAKE A LIST

List particular times and situations that give you special pain and trouble in your bereavement. Continue expanding this listing over several days. Later, read them over and look for some common denominator. It is best to discuss this list with someone you trust and respect.

Don't berate yourself for not feeling as much pain as you first did. Sometimes we tend to be anxious about what may feel like too rapid or even too slow a recovery. The healing process makes us stronger and better, but it takes time, love and lots of patience.

Moving On

"Goodbye My Loves."   *Courtesy, HartsdaleCanine Cemetery, Inc.*

Mariposa and Rose Marie.
  Courtesy, Hartsdale Canine Cemetery, Inc.

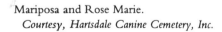

10

Another Pet?

"A friend is a present you give yourself."
—Robert Louis Stevenson

THERE ARE many people whose personalities are ideal for owning a pet. They make the best companions and owners. The relationship they create with their pets is one of great mutual love and trust. In this instance, pet and human lead an enhanced, happy life together in a marvelous symbiotic relationship. Each partner gives and gets, in deeply personal ways that are only beneficial. Such a relationship can be enriching beyond description.

Usually, these people are the ones hardest hit emotionally when the pet dies. And there will be a time during the initial bereavement period when even these "naturals" are not yet ready for another pet. It is almost a sure thing though that they will want another one someday. But when?

READINESS

Timing is everything when considering this. You must be ready for the relationship, or the new pet may suffer because of your underlying resentment. Sometimes we may well be prepared, but hesitant or even fearful. It could easily feel like betrayal to the deceased pet, even though it really isn't. Indeed, resentment or even outright rejection may follow if the replacement is made too soon. Most people need to be alone for a while with their memories. Remember, children are people, too. If they are not too young, let them in on the underlying thinking and the decision-making process as well.

A new pet can represent a healthy continuation of life when you are ready. Another side benefit is that it opens a means to meeting new people. We become socially exposed when we walk a dog, buy pet food in the store, have membership in a pet club, etc. The walk also provides us with some well-needed exercise. We get out of the house and break the grip of isolation. However, being forced into a premature new pet relationship is another problem, and one that can be very upsetting.

Testing Readiness

Good advice is cheap, easy to get and usually well intended. But in the emotionally charged subject of resolving your personal bereavement, no one else really knows your feelings and responses to the suggestion to get another pet. Even you may not be sure of your own readiness.

But you may be more ready emotionally than you may have thought at first. Prepare for the next step in helping yourself make a decision on this problem. It will offer a graphic demonstration of whether or not you are ready to have a new pet.

1. Visit an animal shelter. Do this just to *look around, not adopt.* You must be firm with yourself about this resolve. Temptation may be strong for the moment. But hasty, impulsive decisions can be very much regretted later.
2. Write down your feelings after this visit, and read them again at another time. Share them with a trusted friend. What new feelings are you beginning to have now after the visit? Did you retain a strong memory of any of the animals you saw?

82

Sometimes, in exposing ourselves to these needy companion animals, we unconsciously help ourselves break out of the most maudlin part of bereavement. Feeling pity and love for homeless, lovable animals in this kind of situation can stimulate a quicker resolution to our bereavement. It can change our perspectives in a positive way, without pain or argument.

3. We tend to forget the difficulties in rearing a pet. Do you remember how long it takes for a puppy or kitten to adjust to its new home? Do you recall how long it took you to adapt to this, with all the work, frustration, annoyance, anger, time and expense involved? If you are really ready, your experience might well make the new training period easier, who knows?

Children who want an "immediate replacement" should have it explained that there is no such thing. Each animal is unique, especially in personality. The pet is not a toy, and a new one can't be used to substitute for the deceased pet. If they are above the age of four or five, children should experience the mourning period first. Don't try to protect them from this. It can do emotional damage. Speak with them to determine their level of comprehension of the problem.

Many bereaved pet owners feel that their pet represents something that can never be replaced. It becomes a symbolic link to the past, and a sense of one's own continuity and personal history. The thought of getting another pet at this time feels like disloyalty to the beloved memory. During the earlier stages of bereavement it might well be, but this does change, gradually, as the pain eases.

It would mean companionship again. The pet would be glad to be your new friend as well. It would be "someone" to care for. Being responsible for an animal's life again can be a good experience. Death should not scare us away from new life.

When I conduct group support sessions I usually allow my dog to be present. She senses the grief and goes around the circle of bereavers, stopping to love and be loved by each one in turn for a few minutes. It is amazing and gratifying to see how much therapy a little loving animal can give to people in deep mourning for their own pets. She has been hugged, kissed, whispered to and cried over. Almost without exception, I have been told how helpful this exposure was in easing grief.

We can touch and fondle our pets. This is so good for us for many reasons. Pets decrease loneliness and depression. It has been proven that our general health improves by being and interreacting with them. They lower blood pressure, relax our bodies, help improve our resistance to disease and give us amusement and other pleasures as well. It has been clinically proven that they can lengthen the duration of one's life, while improving its quality as well.

Do you have a strong fear of another pet death? If so, would you be able to handle such a loss and bereavement again? *The answer is probably yes.* But you probably should not opt for another pet until you have worked through your present grief and early phases of mourning. No one else can tell you when you are ready.

TAKING THE STEP

Don't rush into this. Sometimes, under extraordinary circumstances, quickly getting another pet is advisable. This is rare, and always has urgent and complicated reasons for its justification.

Some well-intentioned people try to show their love by buying a replacement for the bereaved owner. They can create a major problem by this caring but foolish act. They are, in effect, forcing the bereaved to accept an immediate replacement, well before that person may have been able to work out basic grief. Because we love animals, we may feel sorry for the little orphan, wanting to care for this new pet. That can be especially cruel at the wrong time. It really is foisting one's will upon another who may not yet be ready to make a reasonable commitment at the moment.

If you feel indecisive about getting another pet, don't do it yet. You can be ready only when and if this ambivalence is won over by more positive feelings about yourself and a new pet-friend. Only you will be able to sense when the time is right. Stay with your "gut feelings." Trust your instincts. They have much truth underlying them.

When you finally do decide on opening up your life to another companion animal, there are some basic considerations you should make. If you like the same breed and color, that's fine, but do not try to remake the new animal into a replica of your deceased pet. When you love the memory of a deceased pet, replacement is not a copy. There can be no such thing. A new pet is an individual with a different personality.

The initial period of adjustment teaches you, as well as the pet, about each other. Make a new relationship and build it on mutual trust and respect. This will be your new friend. Get toys that are not reminders to you of your deceased pet's playthings. Give this new pet a chance to be wonderful, too, on its own merits.

Older people may feel they should not get another pet, just in case they become too ill or infirm to continue to care for it. They fear developing a strong bond, and then being guilty of not living up to the responsibility. They also worry about dying before the pet does. This could become too complicated. It also would upset the pet, which wouldn't be fair. If they live alone, that adds to the potential problems.

Sometimes it is an excellent idea to get another pet before the first one dies. It may make good sense to bring home a baby animal friend for the old one, as well as yourself. If the older pet accepts this (and most will) the animal's quality of life remaining will be much improved. This will also have great psychological benefits for the owner, who has "someone" who can share the loss of the older pet when the time comes. Also the owner will not be left alone. There will be another sweet companion animal to care for, and distract from the sorrow.

Remember, a new puppy or kitten will make many mistakes and possibly cause some damage to your property. Perhaps you forgot this. But you must never take out your anger for the previous pet's death when you are so upset, even if provoked by this youngster. This is another loving life, and a completely different set of responsibilities.

Testimony to a dear monkey.   *Courtesy, Abbey Glen Pet Memorial Park*

A monument at Bide-a-Wee for former President Nixon's dog, Checkers.
Photo by George Wirt

Three very different examples come to mind, examples that illustrate interesting problems concerned with getting a new pet.

CASE HISTORY

An unmarried woman in her mid-fifties was referred for therapy by her former pet-food shop proprietor. She held a middle-management position in a large corporation, and was financially secure. She came for help because of constant upsetting dreams about her cat, which had been dead for over a year. It was apparent that she suffered from an arrested bereavement, and was still being tortured by her obsessions.

She was excessively talkative, and rambled on about her relationship with the cat. She firmly believed it had shared company with her during a previous existence in ancient Egypt. She believed she had been a member of the royal family and that the cat was a pet treated as a deity.

Without apparent provocation, the woman constantly complained that she could never share what remains of this life with another cat, who would be just another stranger. This compulsive denial indicated that she had a strong subconscious doubt about her decision.

After nearly a year of very slow progress in psychotherapy, it became apparent to her that she really wanted and needed another cat. In fact, she was desperate for one. It was discussed that the new cat would be a completely different personality, and not a reincarnation of her previous pet. Then, using some mystical means, she excitedly chose a kitten from a local animal shelter. Despite her formerly strong denial, getting another pet was, in this case, the best thing for this still bereaving human.

A married man in his early sixties lost his beloved dog, after fourteen wonderful years of close companionship. He was depressed and morbid, and came for bereavement counseling. After two sessions he was just beginning to get through the initial stages of shock and denial.

Suddenly, his well-intentioned daughter, who does not live with him, took it upon herself to get him another dog. She did this without his knowledge or permission. It was the same breed and color as the deceased pet. She tried to get him a replacement copy.

He was stunned, upset and rather angry at this intrusion into his personal life. Because she left it for him while he was away, he couldn't outright refuse the endearing puppy. He was gruff and apparently indifferent to the pup, but accepted the gift grudgingly. That first day there were pitched battles in the household, and he made an emergency appointment for counseling. He decided to take care of the helpless puppy for the while, until he could get his wits together.

Days later the daughter visited and found the father on the couch, with the puppy delightedly crawling all over him with licks aplenty and tail wagging furiously. He hated to admit to her that the puppy was good for him, but that was too apparent. He acknowledged this in his next counseling session, which was his last.

This might have had a far different ending under other unforeseeable circumstances. The daughter was lovingly motivated, but very easily could have created a monster of a problem. She was very foolish, but lucky.

A woman in her late twenties had a very close relationship with her twelve-year-old dog, who was killed suddenly in an accident. Her childless marriage had been rocky since its start, about four years prior. She suffered intense bereavement for her pet and lapsed into a strong depression. Her husband became impatient, bullying and embarrassing her into going for bereavement counseling.

While she was away from home at her first session, he secretly went out and bought her a nearly identical-looking puppy dog. When she returned home and was confronted by this, she grew so hysterical that the husband became frightened for the first time. She absolutely refused to have anything to do with the puppy, and would not even look at it. She quickly retreated into a state of morbid isolation and acute depression and required immediate professional attention. Of course, the new dog had to be returned right away.

She was aware that she had a long history of emotional instability, and tended to become hysterical when threatened or overwhelmed by demands. It did not take long before she became aware that this incident was triggered by her sense of betrayal to her deceased pet, as well as that of oppression and domination by the husband. There was little mutual respect in the marriage, and she felt too weak to fight back effectively.

Bereavement counseling turned into intense psychotherapy sessions. She soon learned that her deceased dog represented the only real love and security she had left. The dog's death created a sense of lonely helplessness, and it aggravated her already existing feelings of inferiority to her husband and others. Losing control was her only emergency escape. It proved effective this time only in that the husband returned the puppy. He also stopped pressuring her, for the moment, to see and do things his way. But he kept implying that she was too ineffectual to be of any value to herself, especially under stress.

Obviously, this is much more complicated than a simple example of pet replacement. We will not go into the other psychological details and problems. This does illustrate rather graphically that making a decision to get another pet may have very complex and delicate roots. In this example, the arbitrary presentation of a replacement pet proved disastrous.

11

Children and the Death of Their Pets

"There is only one smartest dog in the world, and every boy has it."

—Anonymous

THE BEREAVEMENT of children most often has been trivialized or given inadequate attention and respect. We are too involved with out own adult world of complexities and learned associations. Thus, we presume that it is generally advisable to protect them from this "grown-up" experience, which we, ourselves, find to be very upsetting, at best.

OUR OBLIGATION

It would be a great service to our children if we step out of the restrictive mold of our traditional nonthinking response to death. We have a strong obligation to them to begin their experience and knowledge of death in a constructive manner that is not as evasive and euphemistic as that which we grew up with. Each child, depending on the individual level of development, should be allowed to experience his or her own natural feelings of bereavement.

Children do not respond to death as adults do, unless they have been shown by example to behave this way. Their normal reactions are much more natural, curious and varied. There are several important factors affecting their diverse responses to bereavement. Age and experience, generally, are the best predictors of levels of emotional and intellectual development in children, although there can be great exceptions.

Here, we are very concerned with their ability to handle the major stress of facing death, probably for the first time. Our overly protective tendencies too often prevent them from meeting this experience on their own terms. Because of our own fearful preoccupations with death, we overlook too easily the simplicity of a child's levels of awareness and possible response.

PROTECTING CHILDREN—HOW MUCH IS TOO MUCH?

It is a natural instinct to protect children from facing stressful things in general and death in particular. Parents try too carefully to ease or avoid their children's grief. Generally, young people are not permitted to attend funerals, wakes, burials or even memorial services. Nor are they allowed to visit anyone who may be dying. Children are shielded, and not expected to be able to extend sympathy to others in bereavement.

How then can they learn to have it for themselves, later in their lives, when their loved ones inevitably die? Because of this unnatural protection and interference, they have only minimal contact. They lack the firsthand experience that teaches a realistic understanding of death and bereavement.

Parents can't really hide their feelings from children. They are too intuitive and perceptive. But because of our attempts to exclude them from stressful events in our lives, children may respond in counterproductive ways we do not foresee. Feeling left out, they may secretly feel shame and guilt at not being worthy of your trust. They know when they are not included in what should be a natural family sharing of things, bad or good. Around age five this begins to matter.

The general subject of death is not unknown to children, as they watch movies and television, as well as hear reports from their schoolmates and friends. Depending on their age and experience, they also are somewhat aware of the taboo surrounding death and its discussion. Again, they are excluded, and may feel guilty that this is so. Perhaps they have been "bad" again, and don't remember how or why—as is so often the case with children.

CAN CHILDREN ACCEPT DEATH?

Children are very pliant, and can accept nearly anything if it is presented in simple, trusting ways. Any questions they may ask about a pet's death should be answered as honestly and simply as possible. Too often parents become very awkward or even embarrassed in discussing death, so they oversimplify, use trite euphemisms or even lie to the child. "The dog is visiting someone, way out in the country, but will be back later." "It is in the hospital, but will be back soon." "The pet went on a trip." These are all examples of the lie that will slap back in everyone's face sooner or later.

Parents hope that the child will quickly forget, and not challenge the idea. Too often a sense of betrayal of trust permanently damages the parent's status in the child's perception. That often emerges later on in life as deep resentment and anger, when it is discovered that the parent's avoidance of the truth caused upsetting problems that have been suppressed for years.

Parents will have trouble explaining death if they have a problem with it themselves. Children are very intuitive about this. Fortunately, they are resilient and accepting. Children perceive only as far as their limited understanding permits at that time. Things that are unthinkable to us are frequently glossed over with no problem at all to them. Children should never be lied to about things concerning the pet's death. If the questions so upset you, explain this to the children at a level that they can comprehend.

Children and Human Deaths

For many possible reasons, children may not be able to accept the prior death of a significant person in their lives. When this has happened, there is no resolution. The child is in a state of arrested mourning. Very often the household with a beloved pet presents an emotional time bomb to children with this unresolved problem. They will create a fantasy world with the pet, creating a personalized environment of love and security. If the pet should die also before the child can resolve any underlying problems or grief, a new level of stress will result. This may remain suppressed, or suddenly be expressed as secondary anger and grief, augmented by the first loss. Sudden behavioral problems almost always indicate there is something significant disturbing the child.

EXPLAINING PET DEATH

How do you explain a pet's death to children? Begin by asking what they think it is. Use that level of perception as your basis to start sketching out your answers. Don't try to explain fully. Most people can't anyway. You will be even more frustrated if you try, and children will sense this.

Even if you work very hard at preparing a complicated or thorough explanation of the pet's death, it easily could be beyond the comprehension level of the child's developmental growth. Streamline your ideas, but not to the point of oversimplifying them or making them seem trivial to the child. Ask questions, and base what you say on what you learn from the level of the answers you get. To better understand how the child is responding, get some feedback at regular intervals. Ask the child what is confusing or upsetting about the pet's death. Work on that at the child's level, not yours.

"Oh. All I wanted to know is if Fido is in heaven," may

demonstrate that lengthy and detailed explanations beyond an immediate awareness level and need to understand may be lost on that child. But don't underestimate the child by being too simplistic. This may even be resented. There are so many complicated reasons or explanations for things. We must try to address our discussions about death to each individual's perceptions. Younger children are not so interested in most adult details or logic. Mostly they seek easy, satisfying answers that are addressed to their immediate level of inquiry.

Try discussing pet death with your child. If it is at all possible, do this well in advance of the actual event. Most parents are surprised at the level of the child's awareness, openness and willingness to discuss this, even if it may be very simplistic. Such a discussion, of course, depends upon the level of the child's emotional development and experience. Even if the child doesn't seem to comprehend your strong feelings on the subject, this experience will provide a lesson in respecting these feelings in others.

A large part of our culture's bereavement problems originates from the awkwardness or outright inability of individuals to respond to those in need of supportiveness. This happens because they generally don't know any better. An awareness of death probably had been withheld from them. Any experience or training in bereavement sensitivity had been denied them as children. Now, as adults, they may become defensive, impatient or even critical of anyone bereaving for such a "trivial" matter as a pet.

Children do not accept death as adults would. They perceive things more at their surface values. They also presume, and can blame themselves for bad things that happen to the people they love. It is not unusual for children to feel that they were naughty, and God or someone is punishing them for that.

Children tend to suppress their guilt, fears and negative feelings, because they do not know how to talk about these. Sometimes they are expressed in nightmares. Nightmares come from the repression of frightening ideas. They emerge with a vengeance when restraints are gone during sleep.

"All of God's Little Ones."   *Courtesy, Hartsdale Canine Cemetery, Inc.*

Memorial tree, with individual leaf inscriptions.

Courtesy, Abbey Glen Pet Memorial Park

Simplicity Is Best

It is wise to avoid any possibly lurid or morbid details that concern the pet's death (or death in general). That can be overwhelming for a child. These terrorizing ideas may, in many cases, be misperceptions of things that would not upset the child if originally seen in another light.

Sometimes we are shocked at responses we never expected. It is important never to attempt to trivialize a child's grief as a means to ease it. Cases have been studied in which children may think that this also would be their parents' response if they might die. Trivialization reinforces insecurity.

At a very young age children should not be troubled with complicated explanations or discussions about euthanasia. But they should not be excluded or made to feel left out of family conferences, even at their young levels of comprehension. Let them sense how you respond to the death. They will use your example as a positive, safe role model.

Somehow, they must learn that death is the normal ending to life, just as birth is the beginning. Every living thing experiences both. It should be made clear to children that death can be very upsetting, but it is not bad, nor is it to be feared. Too often an irrational fear of death is implanted in children, and this negatively affects the rest of their lives. If you have strong religious views that help you ease your pain, then share these with the child.

A SPECIAL RELATIONSHIP

Usually, a child has a special relationship with a pet. This is very different from what an adult experiences. In some cases there can be almost a siblinglike attachment or understanding between the child and the pet. Be frank with children at their level of comprehension. Ask questions to get feedback and an understanding of how your attempt at communication is succeeding or not. Share and guide, but don't shield children. If you make it easy for them to ask questions, they will be better able to grasp what they need to know. Don't try to protect children from grief over the pet's death. Children need to suffer some bereavement also to be able to reach their own resolutions of the problem.

Pets can be silly, childlike, playful and joyous. These are perfect companion qualities for children. They can learn trust and love from the relationship, while developing their own maturing self-image. A pet provides a sense of security and continuity when the parents are not present. The animal friend is there for the child, no matter what the trouble, or how badly the child may have behaved. The bond is even stronger after the child has been spanked or punished. The child shares all troubles with a companion animal friend. Pets serve as adoring siblings to children. A child's caring for a pet can give a strong sense of responsibility and self-esteem. This becomes part of the young person's personality and attitude toward life.

What fun children have playing with their pets! There are very many pained adults undergoing psychotherapy who wish they could have had such a comfort and release. Children are not inhibited by a misapplied sense of dignity that adults sometimes display. A pet supplies total security and love. There are no judgments or criticism. The pet gives a child a sense of complete acceptance, and enriches the self-image because that pet obeys and loves the child. The pet is loyal, and will stay with a child during hard times, when the child is punished or sick or upset about something. In all, the pet becomes a symbol of emotional security in an unsure world.

DIFFICULT QUESTIONS

Some of the questions most frequently asked by children include: "Where is my pet now? Why did Princess die? Is she happy now? Who takes care of her now? Will I ever see her again?" This last question has two possible meanings. It probably means will the child see the pet again *in this life*. You must understand what the child is driving at and needs to know. Too often we answer in ways that do not satisfy the original question as the child meant it.

Examples of bad and misleading answers to the child include such statements as:

1. "Your pet was loved so much that God took the pet back to heaven." The child may think why not him, as well, or other dear members of the family?
2. "The animal doctor made a mistake and the pet died." A child may think that this may happen between people and their doctors, as well.
3. "The pet ran away." This is tacitly understood by children to be untrue or improbable, at best. The child is being excluded from honest communication. Again, such an attempted deception easily leads to distortions in the child's mind that he or she is undeserving.
4. "The pet went to heaven" or "went to sleep forever" can create frightening associations in a child's mind concerning heaven or even going to sleep.
5. "The pet got sick and died." The misperceived notion that dying is a result of getting sick may be promoted during early childhood. Such a concept can be very upsetting. Children and loved ones get sick, too.

Euphemisms such as "The pet was put to sleep" have created frightening associations with sleep or surgical procedures, during which a person has to be anesthetized. Averted meanings and nonliteral expressions can be all too easily misunderstood by a child, who takes things more at their literal and face value. At a young age, their minds do not work as well in metaphors.

Some of the upsetting and unexpected responses by children to the death of a pet have been "I was bad, so my pet was taken," and "If I am good, maybe he will come back to me." This is related to the bargaining phase adults may experience during early bereavement. What happened to the pet may prove to the child that the world is not a safe place. Any such fears of insecurity assuredly will be exaggerated by other stresses experienced by the child. Family discord will certainly worsen any adjustment to bereavement.

A pet's disobedience sometimes causes death by accident. Obedience to authority is always part of any training either for a child or for a pet. Certainly, no child is perfect in rule abiding. All youngsters experience some feelings of shame or guilt at this. It has been discovered in some young children that they secretly fear they may deservedly meet a similar fate like death since they disobey also. Such a personalized response instills an irrational fear in children that may remain with them for a very long time. It may even promote additional negative social behavior, since the child is already guilty and going to die anyway.

There are several suggestions that have proved to be of value in helping a child adjust to the death of a beloved pet. Some possible considerations would include the following:

1. A ceremony for the pet, which includes the children, helps them bond closer to the parents. This need not necessarily be at the grave site. It serves to include them in a positively structured bereavement activity. Shared rites and rituals on a very personal level help put the grief and death into some greater objectivity. Such an experience strengthens children's sense of family and self-reliance during the mourning process. It also can aid in immunizing them from some of the scary, unspoken subjective confusions of death they will eventually run into.

2. Reminisce, fondly, with the children about the pet. Use pictures, if possible. Associate positive, good events with the pet's memory. Emphasize that as long as we remember and love that pet he or she will always be part of us.

3. Ask your local librarian to suggest children's books that include the death of a pet in the story line. There is a growing number of these in print. Perhaps your book dealer can help as well.

4. Discuss with the child the possibility of eventually getting another pet. Emphasize that this is not to try to replace the beloved pet or the memory, as that can never be done. This is to have another animal friend, when the child feels

ready. It is like loving more than one person at the same time. The new pet will be a different one, but the dead one is still loved and remembered. Suggest that maybe, when the new pet is very good, the child could tell the new pet stories about the dead one. They could have been wonderful friends if they lived at the same time.

Ask how the child feels about it and why. Never argue about this. If there is a conflict between your ideas, suggest that you both think it over and discuss it again in a few days or so. *Be supportive but not critical.*

5. Inform your child's teacher of the death of the pet and its effect on the child. Ask for advice. You may get some good suggestions, based on good developmental, educational training. But even if nothing new is suggested, you can feel more secure that the teacher will be paying special attention to your child's behavior and needs during this period. Ask that the teacher schedule a class discussion about pets and pet loss.

6. Visit an animal shelter with the child. Explain in advance that you will not adopt any animal during this visit. You are going for the special experience only such a visit can give. Encourage the child to ask questions and make comments on what you both see. Discuss this visit later. This will help put the child's grief and needs into a much more objective perspective. That will ease the bereavement considerably.

7. The child should have an opportunity to ask your family's veterinarian questions about the pet's death. You should be present to understand and add supportiveness when needed.

8. In instances where euthanasia is necessary, include the child in a family discussion. Share and explain your thoughts and feelings. Explain to the child that different people react differently to this loss. Each of us needs space, TLC and respect for our personal pain.

The death of a beloved pet presents problems even for a well-adjusted adult. The child, who is completely inexperienced, looks to us for guidance in word and deed. Too often we are at a loss, ourselves, and may lose perspective on the consequences of our behavior during this stressful time. Special care should be taken to be open, supportive and especially loving to the child during what amounts to his or her bereavement as well.

A comprehensive essay on children and the death of their pets would take a book to do it justice. This relatively short chapter is not an attempt to be all-inclusive. Considerations that may have been omitted are not necessarily of lesser importance. As in all studies of a psychological nature, there are so many possible varieties of experience and response. There may well be pertinent problems not dealt with in this somewhat brief chapter.

The ultimate consideration here is that you are always the authority, as well as the role model. See to it that the child feels included in your confidence. Treat the death of a pet with understanding, love and care, allowing the child to benefit from your example. Since, for various reasons, death may be frightening to some children, this tender experience may well help your child endure the death of a significant human at some later date.

He or she sees tears and grief, and learns firsthand what bereavement means. This can sensitize children to the needs of others as well. Don't try to pretend or protect them from reality. Let them share your feelings to a reasonable degree, according to their maturity and ability to understand. Share your experience and general responses with them, but always bear in mind that *you* are the example of how they are to behave. Avoid the mistakes that were made in your life concerning the understanding of death.

12

Euthanasia

"To every thing there is a season, and a time to every purpose under the heaven: a time to be born and a time to die."
—Ecclesiastes iii, 1

THE ONLY POSITIVE VALUE of euthanasia is the necessary and humane relief it offers in shortening either suffering or a very negative quality of life. This choice is highly subjective and often difficult. Consideration of euthanasia is part of the ultimate responsibility of all pet owners. When we own a pet, we are pledged to protect and support the life of that pet. Yet any compassionate necessity to end its life must be addressed. Unfortunately, some pet owners and their veterinarians abuse this sacred trust.

Choosing euthanasia is almost never an isolated option. From our earliest days as guardian of a pet, most of us have thought about it at one time or another. We have thought and in various personal ways unconsciously prepared for this possible need and eventuality. But all that thought is only an abstraction before the grim reality.

THE RIGHT THING TO DO?

Euthanasia may be not so much a matter of being the right thing to do as a psychological nightmare of confusion, guilt and responsibility. To opt for it, you must truly believe that this is the only recourse to a pet's pain and suffering. Once accepted, be steadfast in its correctness for your beloved pet.

The fear of death and loss of the pet can be immobilizing. The anticipation of this can be so overwhelming that one may give in to putting off the necessary decision making. The pet may suffer more than the owner at times like this. Fatal accidents and death while undergoing surgery take the responsibility from us. Otherwise, we must exercise this ultimate trust and bounden duty.

To some people, the decision to employ euthanasia is a convenience, and as easy and simple as throwing away an unwanted toy. To others it is a desperately necessary decision they want but cannot manage to carry through.

Fortunately, most of the rest of us fall somewhere between these two extremes. To choose euthanasia is probably one of the most upsetting decisions you will ever have to make. But to own and care for a pet, one must accept the dreaded responsibility of someday possibly being forced into making this choice.

SEPARATING EMOTION FROM NECESSITY

As difficult as it is, we must try to separate emotion from the decision-making process when contemplating this necessary alternative.

Keep in mind that there are three basic considerations to the awesome subject of euthanasia: practical, ethical and psychological. In most cases they are all vitally interrelated, and each of them can be overwhelming. From the practical point of view, euthanasia may be the only answer to humanely terminating the negative quality of the pet's life.

In the extreme example of a dog turning vicious, there is very little, if any, leeway for an alternative choice. Another practical consideration can be that the owner may not be able to bear the overwhelming emotional stress this situation can cause. Nevertheless, the psychology of the situation still agonizes the owner—who in many instances may dwell excessively on some aspect, creating a strong sense of inadequacy and guilt. In all cases, however, the decision making is subjective, upsetting and unique.

Ethical as well as practical considerations clearly indicate that once the necessity for euthanasia of your pet is accepted, the question should no longer revolve around *if* it should be done, but *when*. The psychology involved in making such a life-death decision is always upsetting, and sometimes the decision is more easily made with the support of people close to you. Often it is wise to get professional guidance or counseling if this decision proves very disturbing.

The Children's View

Children should not be overprotected. They must not be made to feel left out of what could be very important to them. Their love of the pet should be shown to have some weight with parents. Depending on their age and ability to reason, they should be made part of what they feel is the decision-making process. Even if you have privately made up your own mind on what is to be done, make them feel they have contributed good ideas to the discussion. Gentle persuasion is the rule here, not argument. That can cause emotional scars that definitely will last a lifetime.

OPTIONS AND OPINIONS

At what point does the quality of your pet's life degenerate to the critical point where you have the ethical responsibility and obligation to end it? This is a terrible crisis for both you and the beloved pet.

Certainly, you should consult your veterinarian and others whom you trust to give objective, sound advice. One sometimes hears the suggestion to refer to an additional veterinarian for a second opinion. Although this has some merit, most practitioners will ask what the first one had said and will usually agree.

As painful and difficult as it is, the final decision must be your own. In considering euthanasia, its value is already accepted. But the decision must never be arrived at hastily. *Once acted on, it can't be reversed.* This is a terrible heart-wrenching conclusion that has to be fully confirmed in advance. Once chosen, it must be embraced as truth and finality.

What are our options for euthanasia during a medical emergency? If the pet is in terminal pain or dysfunction, we owe that pet the dignity of a painless and dignified death. Since death is imminent anyway, we can be more philosophical about it, and accept it a little earlier. Is there any realistic chance of spontaneous recovery or a cure? Will the animal's suffering increase? Are the medical expenses *absolutely* prohibitive? What about the protracted emotional strain on you as well?

In considering euthanasia we are going through an intensely shocking decision-making period. During this time the veterinarian may use some terms and euphemisms that the pet owner may not explicitly comprehend at that highly confusing and unstable moment. There have been cases in which they have been told that their pet should be "put to sleep" or "put out of its misery." These were agreed to without the full understanding at the moment of what it meant. The intense guilt and anger that resulted from these instances could have been avoided. When we are very upset we frequently do not comprehend metaphors well. We are more literal-minded, and may miss the point entirely. This is another strong case against the use of euphemistic terminology and clever avoidance of reality.

Even when the word *euthanasia* is used, there sometimes are emotional blockages that interfere with its full understanding. In a denial of this immediate reality we can set ourselves up for a terrible aftermath of guilt and soul-wrenching grief. We must be on top of the situation. It may be advisable to have someone you trust with you when asked for a decision on euthanasia. Later it is too late to change your mind. The suffering, terminally ill pet may be ready for it, but is the owner?

"Enriching Our Lives."   *Courtesy, Hartsdale Canine Cemetery, Inc.*

The expression "putting an animal to sleep" is quite literal, in addition to being one of the euphemisms usually used for very uncomfortable situations. The veterinarian painlessly injects a massive overdose of sedative or barbiturate intravenously. Some practitioners employ two different injections. Whatever suffering or discomfort your pet may have been experiencing up to that point is eased and released, as the animal quickly slips off into peaceful sleep and death.

As terrible and difficult as it is for each pet owner, most choose to be present for this simple, final procedure. They prefer to hold the pet in their arms, calming the animal, expressing their own final loving farewells and tears. The moment is so intensely personal and emotional that it often becomes overwhelming.

Here, comfort is sacrificed for the last testimonial to their lives together. Intense personal grief is the price of this necessary humane action. However, it is not uncommon to hear that this special moment together is experienced as a very spiritual, loving, transcendent episode. Many report that this unexpectedly gave them a profound quieting sense of completion. So it may well not be so dreadful after all.

If you opt for this as an act of mercy, it is good to close the book well. Say your personal, tearful good-byes. Understand that there is a unity in all things. When you die, your oneness with your beloved pet will be even more complete. But for now it must be over, except in your heart.

Yet there are people who cannot bear to experience this, and there should be no shame in that. Witnessing the moment of death is far too upsetting for some. Unfortunately, it is not uncommon for some individuals who elected not to be present during that final moment to later regret the decision. They worsen their bereavement with a confusion of guilt and additional irrational reasons for grief. Opting to be present or not is a very painful and important decision that should take into consideration what is best for you as well.

Most veterinarians find this procedure upsetting to perform, despite their frequent need to use it. A few, however, have developed an office rule that the pet owner may not be present during the actual process. Experience has taught them that people can suffer from a variety of unexpected strong emotional responses.

Also, there is the real business concern for financial liability. Some owners may faint, hurting themselves in the fall. Others might get hysterical, grow irrational or destructive or even suffer a heart attack from the unusual stress. It is best to discuss this first with your veterinarian and ask for advice. If it is necessary, you may have to choose another veterinarian for the procedure. But *you* should make the decision.

AN OBLIGATION

In being the "provider of all things" to your pet, you have assumed a godlike role. From your pet's point of view, you are the cause of all that pet understands. In addition to the love the pet knows, this includes everything from obedience, tricks, and toys to food, medical care, shelter, company and every experience it has had.

But, as stated earlier, with this role you also took on the awesome responsibility of someday possibly having to make that final decision of life and death. As much as you don't want to have such an obligation, you do. There is no one else who has this individual moral and legal responsibility to decide or act accordingly. You must make that informed decision, and be able to live with it later. And you have to be absolutely right in your conclusions, out of love for your pet as well as concern for yourself. Later on, this must not be distorted in some neurotic challenge to your self-respect. The decision is always painful and fraught with emotional pitfalls.

It is regrettable, but organized religion generalizes and euphemizes about this relatively new problem of the death of pets, sidestepping the lack of real answers. We are forced to make religious interpretations that fit the times but have no biblical precedent. Even if you are religious, what is wrong with "playing God" during an emergency if God doesn't act? Perhaps the deity sees it as your responsibility. There are many who now believe that the moral requirement demands humane action from the divinity within each of us. Chapter 15 of this book makes an innovative breakthrough in this problem.

A PERSONAL DECISION

Before resorting to euthanasia, it is helpful, if time and circumstances allow, to consult as far in advance as possible with a few trusted friends or family, as well as at least one veterinarian. Ultimately, however, this decision must be made subjectively in the deepest, most private, inner soul-searching you are capable of. The intimacy of your relationship with your pet may demand that no one else can be part of this intense personal morality. *But what should be absolutely foremost in your mind is the terrible negative change in the quality of life of your pet.*

Postponement may provide some more time for you, but is that the proper concern? That can be really just another way of trying to avoid and delay the inevitable. Such a stay is only temporary, at best, and may only be serving a self-defeating denial of the grim reality of pain and sadness. Thus, the practical aspect usually helps make the decision for us. It then becomes a matter of logistics and subjective horror. If this must be, then respect it. Honor your pet and yourself in this ultimate private salute to the animal's life with you; have it done quickly.

Not Just a Way Out

Too many pet owners use euthanasia as an easy way out of an uncomfortable stewardship. Unfortunately, they resort to this procedure to terminate the life of an animal without medical problems, one that just does not behave the way they want it to or causes problems. Sometimes this is decided on because people just don't want the pet any longer, and that seems better to them than abandoning the animal or giving the pet to an animal shelter. There are qualified pet ethologists and trainers who could remedy most problems if consulted. But, of course, there are all sorts of people, as well as varied responses to situations. Because you cannot be spared from making this ultimate consideration, it is probably the most distressing action you will ever have to take. Always bear in mind that no one else can legitimately pass judgment on you for deciding on euthanasia. They should respect your grief and painful decision with silence or supportiveness. If there are some in our lives who are critical, we must be able to ignore them or correct them or discard them. This is essential for our own sake, as well as that of the loving, living memory of our pet. Beware of hasty, emotional overreactions to these people though.

ETHICAL CONSIDERATIONS

From the ethical point of view, do we have the right to take life? In the animal and pet world, this was settled long ago in the name of humane action. But it is argued that life is life, and the life of a beloved pet is in many ways equated with our own.

Because there are still many who feel that we do not have the right to euthanize ourselves, the argument is weakly carried to pets. It is interesting to note, however, that in the history of American laws concerning cruelty to children, essential new statutes were passed only on the strength of already-existing laws protecting animals. These were the necessary legal precedents. We protected our animals better than we did our own young.

In the last few years euthanasia has started to become a high-profile new issue for our own self-treatment. Paradoxically, although "humane" action was originally intended for animals, not humans, there are still some who would not allow any change if they could. Whatever decision you make, if considering this necessary alternative, be sure it is your own. You will have to live with it after it is too late to change your mind. There always will be some who would criticize you, despite their lack of qualifications. Let reality and compassion guide you in evaluating the situation and need for euthanasia.

Legitimacy and Legality

The concept of the living will is only a modern social phenomenon. The writer of such a document is, in effect, giving legal permission to be euthanized—given specific dire medical circumstances. We have all read or heard of instances where people were kept on life-support machines for years, while actually being brain-dead or terminally comatose. The living will gives the individual some measure of protection in being able to decide how to die with dignity.

Shouldn't this respect also be exercised for our dear pets as well? Who else but the loving pet owner has the right or responsibility to make the judgment to involve euthanasia? The word *humane* takes on even stronger meaning in this context.

With the proper ethical safeguards and conditions, euthanasia is legal, as well as the most humane and moral ultimate decision we can make for ourselves and our beloved pets, which may truly be extensions of ourselves. We are now witnessing the recent curious social phenomenon of increasingly new cases of people who are writing living wills for themselves—only after first experiencing the soul-wrenching ordeal of having to euthanize a beloved pet.

In the final analysis, if the decision to euthanize a pet is made for the right reasons, there can be no legitimate challenge to its morality and ultimate ethical nature—even from the narrowest of religious or even bigoted interpretations. Is it not vile and immoral to accept and perpetuate pain and suffering? Is the decision to euthanize a pet less necessary or moral than that for a human? Can we ethically sidestep this responsibility?

Sometimes we experience a delayed reaction. Perhaps the least considered and the most striking effect of having euthanized a pet is the sudden onset of unexpected negative psychological consequences upon ourselves. Being human, we suffer and are bereft at the death of a loved one. But we also can create torment to our lives, and that is a mistake.

There are instances of people later regretting having agreed to euthanasia while they were under great stress. This should be

This memorial statue, by French sculptor Jules Moignez, entitled "Pointer Marking a Pheasant," was valued at $25 when purchased by Geraldine Rockefeller Dodge in 1921. Valued at over $4,000 in 1976, it now graces the entrance to St. Hubert's Giralda, an animal shelter, museum and education center on the grounds of the former Dodge estate in New Jersey. *Courtesy, St. Hubert's Giralda*

an informed decision, made beforehand or after a reasonable waiting period. In some instances, whether or not the decision was a good one is not what really matters now. The bereaved pet owner can be ambivalent, insecure and lacking emotional stability because of the pressures at the moment. Often, there are other underlying reasons for this, with secondary guilt usually the most common one.

A RATIONAL RESPONSE

We all respond individually, and sometimes irrationally. The death of a loved one will put us into mourning. Whether the end was spontaneous or humanely produced, the human equation is not changed. Because of the intensity of our emotions, clarity of thinking is usually lost for a brief while, as the confusions of guilt often distort our lives. Guilt is one response to accepting responsibility but not being able to bear up under it.

The subject of death has always upset, intimidated and confused us. Who is to say what it really is or what it means? That frightening grasp for insight into the unknown for assurance, reunion and justification must ever evade us in our all too human fragile nature. Being forced by love and morality to become the angel of death for our pets is often overwhelming, or unsettling at best. But it serves two necessary and good purposes: We do what is best for the pet, and we ourselves are forced into an enormous existential growth step. We go on.

Those who most terribly suffer this role frequently have created their own pitfalls by becoming too emotionally dependent on their pets. Intimate life-styles and complex psychological interdependencies affect each of us in different ways and degrees.

Most often the beloved pet becomes an unconscious symbol of a deep personal need or inadequacy, which finds fulfillment in some degree of fantasy. We allow our animal friends to give us some private transcendence. This is not at all unusual, but seldom recognized and even less admitted.

All humans experience some neurotic needs, each one so very

personal and unique. These responses can span the spectrum from harmless to pathological. The real measure of our "normalcy" is determined by how we respond to stimuli, while maintaining what we have determined, individually, to be our usual life-style. Since our pets become extensions of ourselves, their innocence in such a world of troubles often represents the good part of ourselves, which we inwardly love and isolate. This constant supportiveness from a pet is, in a reasonably blameless way, a small escape from reality. The interrelationship between master and pet often becomes a living exercise in creative fantasy, as well as improved self-esteem.

ONE FINAL CONSIDERATION

As touched on earlier, one final consideration in the decision process has to be made here.

There are some unique situations where the pet's degenerated quality of life may not yet be fatal. But the extreme heroic measures that are required to maintain this strained life could prove too oppressive to the pet owner emotionally or financially. That, too, becomes a valid and legitimate consideration in whether or not to euthanize at this point. At what time may pet owners stop sacrificing their *own* quality of life to temporarily stave off the inevitable? Again, only the individual may make a legitimate judgment on this.

By having to become the angel of death to that beloved pet and extension of ourselves, we are each tasting a bit of our own death, which is always upsetting. We are realistically forced back into the aloneness of our life journey, despite all the friends and family we may have.

In having to euthanize, we must come to an existential turning point in our lives—ever seeking personal understanding and justification. In meeting ourselves in this darkness, we learn that we can go on. We are strengthened by that particular living, loving enrichment with the beloved pet we were so fortunate to have shared for a few years. We have to be better persons because of that wonderful experience of being the loving guardian of a dear pet and now its memory.

DO THE ANIMALS KNOW?

Some owners fear that their pets know what is going to happen when they take them out on that final trip, or call the veterinarian to the home. They may sense their time has come, and that the owner is helping them. There have been reported cases in which a pet that was about to be euthanized showed signs of being greatly upset because the owner was in another room. In each case, when that person joined the pet and veterinarian, the animal grew very calm, and waited to be helped out of all pain and misery. It seems they need us for the parting.

The pet may recognize the veterinarian's office, and demonstrate whatever anxiety previously had been associated with it. Also, an animal will be sensitive to the owner's intense feelings at this time. So far as we know, with the exception of only the higher primates, animals are not upset at the prospect of their own deaths. When their time comes, they sense it, and often go off by themselves, accepting death as normal. They do not get morbid or sentimental about it. Only humans do that. But we find this difficult to accept, and embellish or distort the reality to make us feel better.

Our pets do not get upset at the prospect of their own deaths. That is a figment of our own imaginations, and has become one of the more unnerving misperceptions that people have. When we "anthropomorphize," we are romantically attributing human qualities to pets, which do not belong. The nearest behavioral trait to this, which some animals display when they sense that they are dying, is to become quiet and go off somewhere to be alone.

But there is no regret or sadness in their minds. Those feelings are ours, exclusively, in our pet relationships. We should not torture ourselves during our grief by worrying about this and distorting our final memories of the pet.

116

ADDITIONAL THOUGHTS ON EUTHANASIA

What about proposed slaughterhouse reform? Don't we have a moral obligation to act to remedy these daily horrors?

Have you become aware of the rapidly increasing trend to vegetarianism? Why are so many people switching from the eating of animals?

Did you ever think that even the bait worm screams on the hook, but you can't hear it—and won't allow yourself to observe or even acknowledge its agony?

If an individual is not involved in these and similar considerations, then the argument can be made that that person has little or no moral right to oppose euthanasia.

Much of the world remained passive to the Nazi holocaust while it was rampant. The same horrors are being committed today in many countries. If we can turn away from these, preferring "studied ignorance" and to be noncommittal, then where is our right to ethically judge or condemn euthanasia?

It is never too late to become involved, to become an evolved human. The movement grows. Each of us grows. The life and death of all animals is our moral concern. This includes pets, and humans as well.

In our grievous encounter with death we can learn new things. But there are answers to some personal problems about pet death and bereavement and euthanasia that cannot be answered by this or any other book.

A devoted pet ever mourned.   *Courtesy, Hartsdale Canine Cemetery, Inc.*

Ossuary for beloved cremains.   *Courtesy, Abbey Glen Pet Memorial Park*

118

13

Final Arrangements

*"Break, break, break at the feet of they crags, O sea!
But the tender grace of a day that is dead will never come back
to me."*

—Alfred, Lord Tennyson

IT IS PART of your responsibility to make final arrangements for your pet. Most veterinarians can take care of this for you, if that is your decision. There are several options available. Thinking about these options well before the actual time of death is always preferable. It will help to provide you with a factual and rational decision, not one made under intense pressure. This also offers a minimum of possible mistakes and later self-recrimination.

But if you are faced with the need to make an immediate decision, delay it at least for a few hours. Talk with trusted, concerned people. Ask them about their feelings and opinions. However, be sure your final decision is your own, regardless of who agrees with it or doesn't.

If you should have a reasonably strong feeling about what action to take, don't hesitate. Put it into effect right away. You are likely to get all sorts of conflicting and ill-advised opinions later. What other people think should be of lesser value than your own feelings and considered decision.

BURIAL OPTIONS

In the option to memorialize a grave, there are a few burial choices you may consider. Interment has been practiced since the beginning of recorded history, and probably well before that. Many graphic records exist from classical Egyptian times of hieroglyphic writing containing mummified dogs and cats.

Today there are many pet cemeteries throughout the world. Most of them seem to be in the United States, however. As a rule, these are spacious, beautifully landscaped and legitimate. They also take pains to provide legal safeguards for grounds-keeping, as well as having provisions against the land being reused in the future for any other purpose.

Private cemetery costs vary from a few hundred dollars and up, accordingly. The option of community burial is offered by many pet cemeteries and humane societies, such as the Bide-A-Wee Foundation. Such organizations provide similar memorial facilities that are considerably less expensive, while preserving the dignity of your pet's memory. Your veterinarian should be able to advise you about this. Otherwise, it may be wise to contact your local SPCA office for advice.

Cremation First?

Cremation is another option. This is becoming more popular as a choice for humans as well. At the present time, about 45 percent of pet deaths are treated in this manner. It has some advantages you may wish to consider.

1. Most humane societies, as well as pet cemeteries and some veterinary clinics, operate their own crematoriums. They usually provide informative brochures that you should obtain well in advance of any need for their use. The choice of individual or communal cremation is explained.
2. Generally, fees range from $75 and up for individual cremation. Communal cremation is much less expensive. The size of the pet is usually the major factor in determining cost.

120

3. Most veterinarians can be your go-between in this as well. They will handle all the details that may prove too upsetting for you, the bereaved pet owner, at the time. In individual cremations you are always given the option to have the ashes to keep or deal with as you choose. This is not possible if you elect mass cremation with other pets.
4. The ashes, sometimes called cremains, may be buried the same as a body. Some cemeteries reserve special sections just for this type of interment, however. Others will allow either type of burial anywhere on the premises. It was interesting to learn that in most states people may have their own ashes buried along with those of their pet or pets. The law is not so restrictive in the burial or disposal of cremains.

PET CEMETERIES

At present, there is only one pet cemetery in the United States that has adjacent plots for pets as well as their owners—the Bonheur Memorial Park, in Elkridge, Maryland. Most states and communities outlaw this practice. Indeed, in most areas people may not even bury a beloved pet on their own private property.

Telling the Bad from the Good

Caveat emptor! "Let the buyer beware." You should know that there are some pet cemeteries and mortuary facilities that are run by unscrupulous, unfeeling people. These few scoundrels deliberately mislead and cheat the trusting pet owner, who unfortunately is not in any position to objectively evaluate each service at the time of bereavement. This aberration of an otherwise honorable profession has been prosecuted in court and found guilty of violating many laws. They are con artists, deliberate criminals who prey on very vulnerable people at a vulnerable time. But they get rich quickly as a result of their vile scams.

In 1991 there was a scandal involving a pet cemetery in Long

Island, New York. Trusting mourners who believed their pets were buried or cremated according to contract were shocked to discover mass burial pits containing the decomposing bodies of beloved pets who were supposed to have been treated in completely different ways. The cemetery owners were tried and found guilty on many counts of criminal behavior. They are being sued in civil courts as well by thousands of bereft pet owners. Although these criminals are at the time of this writing serving jail terms, the irreversible damage has been done. Admittedly this is a rare example, but it may not be the only one.

It would be completely wrong to brand the entire pet mortuary profession with the same stamp. Most of these are very legitimate businesses with fine reputations. Some have been in existence nearly a century. They are eager to prove their legitimacy. In choosing an appropriate cemetery, the responsible pet owner should do some thinking and investigation beforehand. Most families have burial plots already assigned to their still living members. This makes sense with pets also.

There are many very fine and distinguished pet cemeteries widely distributed throughout the United States. For more information on what is available in your area, it is best to ask your local veterinarians, as well as other pet owners who have used these facilities. These are also usually listed in the telephone directory Yellow Pages under "Pet Cemeteries and Crematories." Information is also available free, on request, by writing to the International Association of Pet Cemeteries, Carolyn Kinsey-Shea, Exec. Director, 2845 Oakcrest Place, Land O'Lakes, FL 34639. Or you might call this association at (800) 952-5541.

Visits

Visit any pet cemeteries that are in your vicinity. Walk around. Look and feel how other loving pet owners have felt. Read the inscriptions. You will be moved and strengthened by them. It will be an experience of great positive value to you, regardless of how you decide to care for the body.

It is a very moving experience to visit an established pet

cemetery. The varied grave markers, stones and monuments, along with their heartfelt inscriptions, are a powerful testament to our love of all types of pets. Many family burial plots have impressive markers and inscriptions memorializing different pets belonging to the same owner or family over time. Each of these was buried years apart, and the stone inscribed accordingly.

In 1986 a team of archaeologists unearthed a pet cemetery in Ashkelon, a port city of the Persian Empire that had been inhabited by peoples in the eastern Mediterranean in what is now southern Israel. The skeletal remains of about a thousand dogs, from puppies to old ones, were individually buried over a long period of time. This dates back to what is called the Persian Period, which lasted from about 500 to 332 B.C. All signs indicate that each dog freely roamed a sacred precinct and died of natural causes. The plots had been cared for and protected from scavengers and human inter-ference. This unexpected find is the oldest surviving record of a pet cemetery ever discovered.

From ancient Egypt there are even older remains of individual mummified dogs and cats, along with their carved and inscribed sarcophagi.

HOME BURIAL

Perhaps the ultimate in pet interment is the home burial, with a solemn private service, as well as a monument. Usually this kind of interment is permitted in rural and some suburban settings. Check first with your local municipal government to ensure that this is not prohibited by law in your area.

THE FINAL DECISION

Whatever your final decision, burial or cremation, hold some sort of private service for your beloved pet. You will keep good, permanent memories of this. Only those friends and family who would appreciate such a ceremony and would want to be there

123

should be invited. Children definitely should be made to feel they are a basic part of this. It is a practice that has proven to be one of the healthiest beginnings of the mourning process.

Such a private service will help you understand your underlying feelings, with a dignity and pride you probably couldn't have appreciated before. It need not be of any traditional religious nature. Its purpose is to express your spiritual values in a loving retrospective. A few personal words from each person present, followed by your eulogy, should be sufficient. That is up to you.

Text Taken from a Memorial

". . . For if the dog be well remembered, if sometimes she leaps through your dreams actual as in life, eyes kindling, laughing, begging, it matters not where that dog sleeps. On a hill where the wind is unrebuked and the trees are roaring, or beside a stream she knew in puppyhood, or somewhere in the flatness of a pastureland where most exhilarating cattle graze. It is one to a dog, and all one to you, and nothing is gained and nothing lost—if memory lives. But there is one best place to bury a dog.

If you bury her in this spot, she will come to you when you call—come to you over the grim, dim frontiers of death, and down the well-remembered path and to your side again. And though you may call a dozen living dogs to heel, they shall not growl at her nor resent her coming, for she belongs there.

People may scoff at you, who see no lightest blade of grass bent by her footfall, who hear no whimper, people who have never really had a dog. Smile at them, for you shall know something that is hidden from them.

The one best place to bury a good dog is in the heart of her master . . ."

Anonymous

124

14

Supportive Counseling

"Sweet are the uses of adversity."
—William Shakespeare

IT OFTEN has been said that the grief period for the death of a pet can even be more difficult than for a human. At a first superficial glance this may seem strange. But there are many bitter and sarcastic people around who would leap at any opportunity to try to make anyone else seem foolish. Obviously, they have a deficit of understanding to start with. At a time of grief and bereavement we have enough real trouble and don't need more, especially when it is a mean-spirited expression of someone else's problems.

As mentioned a few times in this book, our culture has a strong bias against close attention to the many possible meanings of death. We make a studied practice of avoiding any such considerations, unless they become absolutely necessary and cannot be ignored for the moment. It makes us very uneasy, tense and even scared to face this subject. So we customarily have left this odium to the traditional "death professional," the clergy and morticians. They are trained and experienced, and will do part of each person's job in facing death. They guide us as we avoid our own individual existential accountability.

INDIVIDUAL RESPONSES

Each of us is unique, an individual with strengths, beauty, flaws and fears. We respond in different ways to everything. One of the things that make our collective humanity wonderful is our natural tendency to join in common goals.

Of course, there are always some antisocial people who express their personal problems as hostility to the collective good. They also seek out the vulnerable individual in a neurotic attempt at self-aggrandizement, trying to bolster their insecurity. They must belittle to feel important.

But people are inherently honorable, and we tend to improve ourselves, individually and in community. Despite some terrible black marks on our history, civilization is generally improving with age.

Sometimes during a period of need and unhappiness we discover positive values within ourselves, which we did not know for sure were there before. This is as true for the individual as it is for a community of people. In our private bereavement we are finding hidden strength and maturity beyond what we started with. One of the modern-day marvels of our contemporary society is that we are beginning to open up our hearts and humanity to each other's needs in many ways. We are initiating new attitudes and actions to better ourselves, as single persons and as members of a constantly improving social structure.

CONCERN FOR OTHERS

There are many good, concerned people who try to help others. To our credit, the ranks of these humanists are increasing. Concern is growing for others and their individual problems.

Within the past decade or so we even have seen a growing

126

"A Gift of Love Memorial," testimony to many pets who enriched their owners' lives.

Courtesy, Abbey Glen Pet Memorial Park

Memorial to fire dogs.   *Courtesy, Bide-A-Wee. Photo by George Wirt*

open supportiveness for pet bereavement. This all too human expression used to be socially frowned upon. What we have here really is the beginning of a revolution in thinking and public attitude. Others are beginning to realize that mourning is not a privileged commemoration reserved only for the loss of human loved ones.

Although history and literature provide us with occasional glimpses into personal memorials to beloved dogs, they were rare. These emotional expressions generally have been accepted because of their great human-interest value. The concept is dramatic, even poetic, of a hero weeping for a faithful dog.

As household pets became more common, the problem of pet bereavement increased greatly. This once rare tragedy has become something very different with time. Now we are faced with the misfortunes of the ordinary person dealing with this shock. The novelty gradually wore thin, as pet bereavement became a common experience. Many individuals, however, still tended to hide their distress from those who had no understanding or sensitivity to this problem. As with some other important contemporary social issues, this is coming out of the shadows.

HELP FROM OTHERS

Most often our grief responses need sharing and good counsel. That certainly does not mean that one is in need of professional guidance. If we do opt for trained help, there is no stigma or implication that we are weak or emotionally defective. On the contrary, it may be a sign of good mental health, where we seek answers and objectivity. It just could offer the boost we need in helping ourselves attain some direction during this particular time of trial and suffering.

We need tender loving care and good people around us, at this special time of personal crisis. Anyone who is truly sympathetic can be a good listener. We need people around us, but it is necessary to avoid the company of those who cause stress.

128

There are some helpful practices the person in mourning should consider.

1. If you live alone, try to change your daily patterns slightly.
2. Watch different television programs and listen to other radio stations.
3. Avoid certain types of movies that may be upsetting, and actively seek out others that are entertaining. Enjoy them with someone who is supportive of what you are going through.
4. Although you may feel some initial resistance, arrange to visit or go out more frequently, or even on a regular basis. You can still take memories with you and share them, if you choose.

At this time, avoid situations that may prove upsetting.

Since we are dealing with death here, there should be many available authorities to whom the deeply bereaved can turn for counsel and solace. Libraries and pavilions are filled with such information if the death is that of any human. Our cultural reverence for death takes no notice of whether or not the mourned person was one for whom we had any real concern or even respect. We have been taught to honor the dead regardless. All religions have some preoccupation in this attitude. But now we are asking for help and guidance concerning the death of a beloved pet. Unfortunately, there are precious few answers from theology and its experience rooted in the past.

Religious Teachings

Organized religions have never before been concerned with the death of companion animals. This is understandable since biblical civilization had very few pets, if any, and no need for such considerations. Pets were rare luxuries, exceptions to the norm. Usually they were kept by royalty as a luxury.

Today, the stunned mourner for an animal may feel the need to turn from religion to other avenues for solace and help. But where? Chapter 15 of this book has been designed to help the individual regain some religious perspective and stability.

Counseling

Professionals in psychological and psychiatric training had never considered this before, and the truly understanding counselor is a rare personal treasure. Most counselors with no personal experience or understanding of pet bereavement had offered their general well-intended interest, but it was generally shallow. Now this is finally changing for the better.

Today, the specialty of health and death care for pets has become a multibillion-dollar business. With such increased visibility, it is natural that now there should be some answer to the needs of so many regarding appropriate counseling. Unfortunately, in the past, this had always been rare. Veterinary colleges gave perfunctory instruction or none at all on death counseling and sensitivity. The exceptional humanistic veterinarian was also a rarity. That is all changing.

Within the past decade or so there has been a growing movement to correct this condition and provide for the bereaving pet owner. Veterinary colleges and pet hospitals are now recognizing the need for retraining themselves, as well as the general public. Things are improving indeed.

It used to be that the best chance for getting help was at pet mortuaries, where the sheer volume of varied experiences with bereaved pet owners had created a realistic base of wisdom and philosophy. But they are not really geared for counseling, despite their vast experience. They can help with good, practical advice and supportiveness, but their business is the mechanics of burial or cremation. Indeed, some have hesitated asking for help there because it was felt that the interest of these establishments was strictly that of a financially motivated business. In some instances this is true, but there are a few wonderful exceptions. At least here the bereaved, overwhelmed with grief and despair over a pet's death, have not been looked upon askance.

THE HUMANISTIC VIEW

The growing humanistic view of bereavement has the mourners and their pain as the prime focus, with other considerations as secondary. This understanding is helping to overcome the enormous inertia and stagnation that history has imprinted on our collective social awareness. Times are changing and our values with them, to our credit as a civilization. But this is happening slowly, and not without great labor and pain.

Today the deeply bereaved mourner for a beloved pet has some real help available. At this writing there are at least eight centers across the United States where one now may meet with experienced and trained counselors for this specific problem. Most of them also offer wonderful group support sessions, which are unmatched anywhere by the good they do for pet bereavement. Usually there is no fee as well. These eight are listed at the end of this chapter.

Experienced Professionals

As yet, very few trained professionals in psychology experienced with pets and bereavement have entered this quickly growing field. A few, with considerable experience in pet bereavement, are just beginning to make themselves more visible as counselors. A growing number of other excellent counseling situations are becoming available also. However, they must be sought out.

Take warning though. The newly bereaved are easily duped. Because of the steadily increasing popularity of this kind of counseling, there is always the possibility of a few unscrupulous people who will enter this field for financial reward, without adequate qualifications or experience. Perhaps they will have good hearts and the best of intentions, but that is not enough.

Unfortunately, organized religions may not be able to help, since they are not philosophically or historically oriented in this direction. The rare exceptions lie with a very few variant attitudes. In Catholicism, St. Francis is the patron saint of animals and pets. The individual priest may deal with this as he wishes, each according to personal preference and practicality, in offering solace to the mourner for a pet. There is extreme latitude here, with no major guidelines to define any firm position about whether pets have souls, go to heaven, etc. The compassionate priest who is a real pet lover can be a fine counselor in pet bereavement. But that is only because of a unique personality and approach. He is an exception.

Certain Eastern philosophies and religions hold that all life is precious and intrinsically the same. It is part of the great Oneness of being. Thus the passing of a pet is as respected as that of a human. Here we can find solace in our bereavement for a pet.

Islam, to its credit, respects the souls of all living things. The Old Testament makes no reference at all to pets since they were practically nonexistent, and in biblical accounts, dogs were not used for herding other animals. A strong concern for the humane treatment of all animals is emphasized instead.

For thousands of years, Native Americans have revered life and spirit in all animals, even those they had to hunt.

Certain metaphysical philosophers and transcendental poets offer beautiful hope in this area. They are well worth the reading for inspiration.

Rather than seem pessimistic when viewing the historical record of religion, a detailed study has been made for your consideration. The next chapter is designed to give the reader a more detailed perspective of the positive role that religion may still play in the life and death struggles of the bereaved pet owner. Pastoral counseling, if available during the mourning period, can offer unique and very effective help and hope. But too often, this is difficult or impossible to find. A sense of spiritual uplift is particularly beneficial at this tragic time. Perhaps, by surveying some of the best contemporary religious thought concerning the death of pets, one may find some important insights and self-counsel.

132

Counseling Centers

The Animal Medical Center
New York, NY
(212) 838-8100

Bide-A-Wee Foundation
New York, NY
(212) 532-6395
Wantagh, NY
(516) 785-4199

University of Pennsylvania
School of Veterinary
  Medicine
Philadelphia, PA
(215) 898-4525

University of California
School of Veterinary
  Medicine
Davis, CA
(916) 752-4200

University of Minnesota
School of Veterinary
  Medicine
Minneapolis, MN
(612) 624-4747

Colorado State University
School of Veterinary
  Medicine
Fort Collins, CO
(303) 221-4535

Washington State University
Pullman, WA
(509) 335-1297

St. Hubert's Giralda Estate of Geraldine Rockefeller Dodge
575 Woodland Ave.
Madison, NJ 07940
(201) 377-2295

Bless these pets, O Lord.   *Courtesy, Abbey Glen Pet Memorial Park*

134

15

Religion and the Death of Pets

"A righteous man regardeth the life of his beasts."
—Proverbs xii, 10

TRADITIONALLY, our understanding of and preparation for death had been a subject that fell solely within the province of religion. With the exception of a few metaphysical philosophers, the clergy was the only acknowledged authority on the subject. Historically, however, since the Industrial Revolution our life-styles have been changing dramatically, affecting this situation.

With the onset of a phenomenal growth in the size and population of cities, there was a corresponding decline in rural population. Partly as a result of this, there has been a gradual disappearance of the extended family and a diminishment of the traditional powerful influence of organized religion on individuals. The previously unchallenged regulation of the church over everyday matters was being dramatically affected by the ever-changing socioeconomic condition of the people.

The keeping of pets for pleasure and companionship had originally been the practice of nobility and landed gentry. With the advent of increased wealth and leisure, this natural source of human pleasure began to gain popularity. More and more people were discovering the satisfaction of having a personal pet. Within the span of just a few hundred years, pet dogs and cats were no longer uncommon. At the turn of the twentieth century, New York City had only a few thousand pet dogs. Today there are well over one million, with even more cats. And who can begin to guess at the great numbers of other living things that are also being kept as pets? Of course, the human population has risen as well.

It was inevitable that the dramatic increase in the number of people with pets should result in a heightened public awareness of this relatively new historic phenomenon, the human-pet bond. Gradually, people began to enrich themselves with a close, personal relationship with a companion animal. But they quickly discovered that the pet's eventual death raised passionate questions about whether such a sentient, loving animal had a soul that would find its reward in heaven. In bereavement it is often wondered if, after our own demise, we would we ever join with our beloved pet again in some divine afterlife. The death of cherished animals presented a new problem, which had been ignored or scoffed at, at best—until very recently. Organized Western religion had no established authority or precedent for solace to offer people who mourn the death of their pets. The word "pet" is not mentioned in the Bible or New Testament. Reference is made only to animals in general, with instruction that they should be treated with humane care.

Yet farm animals had always been common, even in biblical times, often sharing the same shelter as their masters. But the harsh demands of survival required that even the most lovable of these animals first serve in their utilitarian functions. Many were raised for slaughter, others for milking. Certain animals, especially their adorable young, must have elicited love and a certain amount of respect from their masters. We find constant instruction in the Old Testament for the humane treatment of animals. But the concept of pets per se was still in the future, and the word *pet* did not yet exist.

All religions with a basis in fundamental interpretation of the

Bible have no literal criterion to deal with anything concerning the subject of pets. But they do refer to the humane treatment of animals. Indeed, there are many religious leaders who believe that only the concern for the life and death of human beings should merit their involvement and responsibility. So where can the pet owner turn for help when the beloved animal dies?

Despite the historic novelty of this problem, there is growing, genuine concern among a few modern spiritual leaders. Humanistic responsibility demands that we care for each other when we are in deep distress. And that caring now is extending to the legitimate, passionate question about the meaning of death for our pets as well. Man has a natural craving for some spiritual guidance and uplift.

It all boils down to the ultimate question: In this modern day, what can organized religion do to help the deeply bereaving owners of pets? Many people have felt abandoned by their religion at this very critical time of their lives They sought wisdom, solace and counsel from the source of traditional spiritual values and they were left without any hope or help. Religious leaders could not offer anything better than generalizations. Where was love? Most of these bereaving individuals may have since turned away, in part or whole, from their religion in deep, bitter and painful personal resentment. Despite whatever lay counsel can be offered, all that we can do is treat the underlying human pain and suffering. A spiritually uplifting perspective is still needed.

Telephone calls, visits and letters went out to leaders of the major religions of the world: Catholicism, Protestantism, Judaism, Buddhism and Islam. After a while it was made evident that those faiths based upon a fundamentalist point of view felt that they had nothing to say about this personal pilgrimage, and would not participate in this endeavor. It was also disappointing that because of their time constraints the Catholic Archdiocese of New York suggested that this chapter be printed without their point of view.

It is with much hope that these considerations are offered here for your reflection and possible spiritual uplift.

THE JUDEO-CHRISTIAN PHILOSOPHY AND THE BUDDHIST VIEW

Judeo-Christian theology is based upon a God of love, who created all things lovingly. In Genesis it is established that we are to care for the rest of God's creations as stewards of the earth. We are to have a loving relationship with all of God's creation. We are obligated to treat that total creation as lovingly as we can, as we know God does. That is part of our responsibility, and what it means to be alive, here, created in God's image.

In the story of Noah we are told, "Behold, I establish my covenant with you, and your descendants after you, and with every living creature that is with you; the birds, the cattle and every beast of the earth with you. . . . This is the sign of the covenant, which I make between Me and you and every living creature that is with you. For all future generations I set my rainbow in the cloud, and it shall be a sign of the covenant between Me and the earth."

God's loving covenant is not made only with humans but with all living creatures. There is a kind of equality established that we must seriously consider. Modern religion is slowly taking up the cudgel of contemporary man's struggle to better understand his bereavement for a beloved pet.

Concern for Pets in the Jewish Tradition

"While Judaism does not address itself specifically to the subject of the concern for or care of pets, it is deeply concerned about the humane treatment of all living things. In English, the principle would be called 'pain to living things.' Animals are a part of God's creation. Humanity has a responsibility to protect them, to avoid bringing unnecessary pain to them, and to treat them without cruelty. Thus, we find a biblical prohibition against plowing with an ox and an ass together (Deut. xxii, 10), on the assumption that the ox, being stronger, would bring pain to the ass. Sabbath laws of rest also apply to the animal kingdom (Exod. xx, 10; Deut. v, 14). From an application of humane consideration it is even forbidden to slaughter an animal and its young on the same day (Lev.

xxii, 28). This same concern is exhibited in such biblical laws as the ones demanding that an animal struggling under too heavy a load have the burden removed (Exod. xxiii, 5), and releasing the parent bird from the nest before taking the young (Deut. xxii, 6–7). Indications of this same consideration for the welfare of animals can be seen in such narrative tales as when the angel rebuked Balaam for beating his beast, an ass (Num. xxii, 23) and when God chastised Jonah for not having compassion for the residents of Ninevah, 'that great city, wherein are more than six score thousand persons . . . and also much cattle' (Jonah iv, 11).

"The rabbinic tradition expanded on the biblical compassion for all living things. One of the seven Noachian Laws (laws that were to be observed universally, not just by Jews) prohibits the eating of the flesh of a living animal. While the rabbis were not opposed to the killing of animals for food, that act had to be performed with the greatest of compassion and speed. It was regulated with strict detail. It was forbidden for a man to eat before he had fed and tended to his animals, and it was out of this same consideration for their welfare that 'a man is not permitted to buy animals unless he can properly provide for them.' The compassionate consideration for the welfare of animals, codified in Jewish law, also finds its expression in legendary material of the Jewish tradition. For example, it is said that Moses and David were considered fit to be leaders of Israel only after they had been shepherds.

"Out of this tradition, it is legitimate to extract an attitude of sympathetic response to the loss of a pet and to the tender administration of a pet's remains. A pet, having brought joy to the life of its owner, is as deserving of loving care in death as it was in its lifetime. However, after its death and disposal, one is not expected to mourn excessively or become involved in bizarre or unnecessarily expensive practices, any more than such expressions would be tolerated after the death of a person.

"Death is a part of life, and after death and reasonable mourning, life is to continue normally as quickly as possible."
—Rabbi Balfour Brickner
Senior Rabbi Emeritus
The Stephen Wise Free Synagogue
New York City

We should consider our personal reaffirmation of the relationship between God and creation. If we are given the particular gift to understand this, then we have the responsibility to help bring it about. We must care for all other living things as well. When any part of that creation dies we must treat that as lovingly as the Creator would. Whenever there is a death in any loving relationship, it must be dealt with in a respectful manner. That is in honor of the loving relationship, which is also God's.

We know what it is to grieve over the loss of something we love. God's love is demonstrated through us, so it is natural to grieve over the loss of a pet, because He grieves over the loss of any life.

Our grief is terrible enough without self-imposed guilt. The necessary taking of a pet's life, in euthanasia, can upset the religious harmony within some people. Despite the dire and demanding circumstances, it could be felt that God's commandment, "Thou shalt not kill," may have been taken in vain. But if the act was truly one of mercy, then God's love was expressed in this performance of duty, and the pet owner is absolved of sin and guilt.

That which we call mercy killing falls into a special category, far from the otherwise sinful act of indifferent killing. We express God's love in preventing any further unavoidable pain and suffering, and actually bestow a personal blessing on the pet. This is, in effect, an intense act of love. Indeed, it is God's love expressed through us in a very disturbing and extreme personal sacrifice. We must wrap ourselves in the beauty and love of that life, keep it with us and go on as better humans because of this.

The Christian point of view emphasizes resurrection and the life that comes out of death. We are taught that the God of creation is always making new life and new relationships. But it is important not to get mired in our bereavement. We must allow the remembrance and understanding of that love to give birth to new opportunity for us to love. We can do this only when we travel through the valley of the shadow of death. The grieving process must be lived through, from beginning to end. We must not avoid it.

140

There is nothing in scripture that suggests any living thing other than man has a soul. To wonder about this is a projection of our anthropomorphic fantasy; we are limited to our human perspective. But it must also be said that there is nothing in the scriptures that *denies* the existence of a soul for any other creature of creation. We are just not privy to God's larger view of truth. One could assume that there is some spiritual dimension to the life and death of other life forms in God's creation. But that would be a personal assumption.

The Hereafter

When we talk about meeting again in some afterlife, we talk about a cognitive recognition that we enjoy in this life. The question of whether we will ever meet again in the hereafter arises out of our involvement with grief and loss. In a sense, it is a fruitless question. It is trying to fulfill an earthly need that will not be a need in whatever life there will be hereafter.

The answer would be truth for tomorrow. But we pose the question as a reflection of the grief of today. We must live into that period of grief and mourning, affirming its value for now. Whether or not one will ever see that pet again is not as important an issue as what one does with the love for and from that pet— and how that love has improved one's life. Such a profound experience should eventually help the bereaving pet owner.

The church would affirm that the real question is how to accept and deal with the pain that comes from such a profound loss resulting from the love of a pet. A funeral is all about putting away the body, saying good-bye to this physical form, and giving thanks for the spiritual. Since nothing is known about the spiritual dimensions of the animal kingdom, most religions do not officially sanction such services for them.

But there are many possible liturgies concerning the death of a pet without getting involved with the affirmation of the spiritual. Pondering whether or not we will ever meet with our beloved pets in the hereafter just doesn't fit into the essential workings of day-to-day life, because that deals primarily with human existence.

We are so involved trying to deal with our daily lives that going off into the much broader spectrum of the rest of creation is fruitless. It is something that most organized religions just have not found the necessity or the time to do.

St. Francis of Assisi, 1182–1226, was a lover of creation. He felt that we are all part of nature, and related. We are one with all of creation. He understood the Creator's love to be for all living things, including man. He believed that God, man and nature were all part of the same truth. Perhaps it was not such a coincidence that Christ was born in a manger, surrounded by animals. There may be a profound metaphor and lesson in this.

The Creator made a covenant with the whole of the animal kingdom, including man as steward. There has always been a strong bond between many of us and our charges. We have come to know there is a capacity for animals to love, and it is natural for us to wonder if they possibly possess some spirituality unknown to us.

Some Episcopal Reflections

"For people of faith, especially of the Judeo-Christian traditions, creation is the living act of a loving God. And for those persons who have special relationships with various members of the animal kingdom, it is important to understand the creatures of this world, big and small, as wonderful manifestations of that creative act. That which is before us, after us, above us, below us, beyond us, within us; that Mother/Father of all life is called by many different names, yet experienced by a majority of the human beings of this earth as that one true origin of *all* life. Plant, animal or human, no matter what the name of the child, one must wonder if it is truly possible for the Mother/Father to care more for one than another. Can the love of the Creator for that which is created be unequally given? I think not, if I am to trust my own feelings as a parent, and am a product of the Creator's will. ('Let us make man in Our image.' Gen. i, 26.)

"The Judeo-Christian tradition leads me and many others to believe in God's love for all living things. It also reminds people

142

of our role as stewards of that creation, of all living things. There-fore, we are to act lovingly to all life, as would God.

"It is natural to grieve; it is the loss of that which is loved. Again and again scripture reminds us that God grieved and still grieves for that which is created when it is no longer truly alive. So it is not only natural but right that, created in God's image, we too grieve when life is lost, any life—all life. It is natural and right to grieve over the loss of a pet that we loved, as God loved. Would the God of love expect anything less of us? I think not.

"There are those who ask the quesion, 'Do animals have souls like ours, and will they be with us in an afterlife?' In a loss situation this question is best heard as an expression of the deep love for that which is lost in death. It is not so important to search for the answer to that which only God knows, as to trust that that which God loved is always under God's care. We, as a people of faith, are our own proof of this comforting truth."

—Reverend Canon Joel A. Gibson
Subdean
The Cathedral Church of St. John the Divine
New York City

A Unitarian-Universalist Perspective

"In the statement of Principles and Purposes of the Unitarian Universalist Association we affirm the inherent worth and dignity of every person, and the interdependent web of existence, of which we are a part.

"In the first of these two affirmations, Unitarian Universal-ism tells us that each one of us has the freedom to decide what is true and right for herself or himself, and the responsibility to act according to these beliefs. In the second we are reminded that what is true and right for each of us must take into account our place in the interdependent web. Both principles can guide us when we are with one who is grieving over the loss of a beloved pet.

"Humans and animals are part of this web—and it is a special strand of love and companionship that links pet and pet owner. Pets are important life companions. They take us out of ourselves by calling us to respond to them, watch them, engage with them. They demand of us responsibility, that we attend to their needs with care. They give to us joy in life, a different perspective, a relief from loneliness, along with their love.

"When that connecting strand is broken—when a pet dies—the resulting feelings of loss are real and significant. And, in that moment, we must attend to the brokenness, guided by the principle of inherent worth and dignity. The person who is grieving knows what the loss means for him or her. And this is the starting point. In our respect for them we can participate in acknowledging the reality of the loss, affirming the feelings of bereavement, of emptiness, in remembering the happy moments, and in learning to say good-bye.

"In the spirit of earth-centered religious traditions, we take time to honor and acknowledge our animal brothers and sisters with whom we share this planet. In the tradition of St. Francis, we set aside a time to bless the animals who are part of our lives. We find ways to celebrate the intertwining of these strands of life. And so it is fitting that we also take time and find ways to mourn the loss and share the grief that the death of a pet brings."

—Reverend Dr. Tracy Robinson-Harris
Unitarian Universalist Community
Church of New York

Eastern philosophy and religious practice has always offered enriched perspectives to the traditional Western ways of looking at things. Although there are many differing sects in Buddhism, Zen being the best known, they all follow the basic teachings of Buddha, each with some variation. In its strange wisdom, the viewpoint offered here can offer hope to the bereaving pet owner. Not surprisingly, it is similar to the Transcendental view of life, widely praised by American and British poets in the middle of the nineteenth century.

144

A Buddhist Point of View

"According to the teachings of Mahayana Buddhism, the main goal of a practitioner is to lead all sentient beings to Supreme Freedom. This is an irreversible state which is free of all suffering and the causes of suffering. It is the state in which the Supreme Bliss is obtained.

"The wish to actually do this is called the altruistic thought of bodhicitta, and is the entrance to the Mahayana path of spiritual development. This altruistic thought has to be arrived at through preliminary practices. First, one meditates on equanimity, which is an antidote to being overly attached to friends—and adverse toward those we perceive as enemies. When one develops equanimity one then meditates on what we believe is a fact, that all sentient beings have been our mother.

"There is no beginning to consciousness; this moment is a continuation of a previous moment of consciousness. Therefore, we all have undergone countless previous rebirths. By this reasoning we can consider all sentient beings as having been our mothers—this applies as well to all animals, including cats and dogs. In their role as our mother they showed us great kindness. We can also observe how animal mothers display kindness in caring for their present offspring. We don't recognize them as our previous mothers because of our new life forms, but they have actually been our mothers, many times.

"Sentient beings are kind to us in all ways, not only in the role of mother. Therefore according to the Tibetan Buddhist tradition all sentient beings, including our domestic pets, deserve our kindness in return. We must do our best to care for their needs and keep them happy and healthy.

"In Tibet it was a custom to purchase sheep and goats who were to be butchered, and then keep them as domestic animals. It was thought that saving the life of an animal was especially helpful when one was ill. Many Tibetans would walk with their animals around temples and holy shrines. Some temples would allow animals inside. Buddhists believe that it is beneficial for an animal to see a religious painting or image or to hear the sound of prayers and teachings. Hearing the sound of prayers and texts is thought to create the cause for an animal to obtain a favorable rebirth.

"When my own cat, 'Jack Benny,' had kidney problems, I bought a cassette recorder. I then played tapes of the teachings of His Holiness, the Dalai Lama, so the cat could hear them repeatedly over several days. I am not the only one who does this. Many people read their daily prayers loud enough for their pets to hear.

"When an animal is dying it is customary to recite the names of the Buddhas and Bodhisattvas to the animal. Hearing these names is especially helpful at the time of death. After the animal has died, holy people can be requested to pray for the deceased pet. One can also go to the temple and make offerings and pray for the animal.

"We believe that in the future all sentient beings can, and in fact will, attain the state of Buddhahood—the state of Supreme Freedom. This is possible because their consciousness is separable from the defilements that currently prevent their attainment of this state. Therefore, every sentient being will become enlightened in the future, when they apply the techniques which separate defilements from their consciousness.

"Of course, it is natural for an animal's owner to suffer and be unhappy over the death of a pet. But as I mentioned before, rather than just being unhappy, the owner can take positive actions to help him or herself and the pet. Say prayers for the pet; do religious practices and dedicate them to the pet. Many religious practitioners remember their deceased loved ones all the time in their daily prayers. They generate and maintain the wish to benefit them, and pray that they will be able to help them obtain better and better rebirths, better and better opportunities for spiritual development—and eventually highest enlightenment."

—The Venerable Khyongla Rato Rinpoche
Tibet Center, New York

As the reader already well knows, there is no simple or single answer to our grief. But the collected wisdom of the ages should be of assistance to us in our search for truths. This chapter is designed to lend some spiritual perspective to the bereaved, regardless of what religion he or she elects to observe or not observe. One may be an agnostic, yet believe that there is some sort of unnamed, all-pervading force within the cosmos. All this offers hope, which is the balm and nourishment we need at this critical time.

Whether we call it by the name *religion* or by any other word, our search for spiritual values and help is a prime force in our human existence on this plane. Each person's personal odyssey, in this search, is a pilgrimage. If the viewpoints offered in this chapter offer some spiritual help in this search, then you are in a position to enrich your life, at least to that extent. The continuity of life is all around us. With hope and time we grow better and better in our own renewing lives.

In memory of all those who have gone before us, and remain in our hearts and minds.

Courtesy, Hartsdale Canine Cemetery, Inc.

148

16

Some Practical Suggestions in Review

"Build thee more stately mansions, O my soul!"
—Oliver Wendell Holmes

1. Let your feelings out. Cry. Don't hold back. This has to come out. The pain and confusion will start to get sorted out. If you suppress this, it will only delay the healing and mourning processes. Sometimes it is advisable to allow yourself some sort of indulgence to loosen up, possibly with a little wine or other spirit, and drink a toast to your beloved pet and the memory.
2. Write a letter or will *from* your pet to yourself. Keep this as a permanent memory. You may be amazed at how much this reveals to you about yourself. Years later this will become a very valuable personal document.
3. Dedicate something in your pet's name and memory. Donations to worthy causes are good. Usually gifts that require a plaque or permanent label give great satisfac-

tion. If your pet was a show animal, then donating a memorial trophy to a pet club is very gratifying. Most humane organizations will appreciate a donation in your pet's name and memory.

4. It is not too late to say something to your deceased pet. Over a period of time, make a list of all the loving memories you have of your pet. Constantly amend this list. Then write a letter to your pet, remembering all these intimate smiles and tears. Keep this as part of your loving good-bye in this life.

But remember, the loving memories live on forever with you, so something of your beloved pet will never die and leave you. Letting go of the pain is not letting go of the loving memories. This list and letter will take on added value with time.

5. Make an audio recording of yourself, reading these memories and saying whatever emotional, private things you feel like adding. Listen to it a few times during your mourning, and add to it whenever it feels right. Keep this as a permanent part of your personal memorial to your beloved pet. You may be surprised at how effective this is when you play it back years later.

6. Establish new routines. Change or vary the old ones. (We fall into the usual emotional reponses when we follow old patterns.) Do things in a changed order as soon as you get up in the morning. At home, try sitting in a different chair or place on the couch. Rearrange your furniture. Work, shop, meditate, attend social functions, walk, jog, run, bike, partake in special events, sports or concerts with other people.

Most importantly, start meeting with people again. Avoid being alone too often. Attend pet bereavement support groups. Regular exercise helps reduce depression.

7. Invite friends, relatives or good neighbors to visit you in your home. Visit other pet owners and their pets. Return (with company?) to some of the sites you shared with your pet. This will help you accept how separate

the past is from the present. You can keep your memories without distorting your experiences, now and in the future. As time goes on, this will become easier.

8. Treat yourself to things you would have liked, but couldn't or wouldn't do before. Imagine your pet's spirit advising you how to ease your pain. Do some enjoyable things with your pet's blessings. Certainly you deserve it. As soon as you can, go on a trip or vacation. If it appealed to you before, now is the right time to seriously consider relocating or changing your job.

9. Avoid keeping visible reminders of your grief. Get rid of your pet's toys and other things you may wish to keep as mementos. If you can't throw them out yet, then put them out of sight in a drawer or a box in a closet.

   Don't make it harder for yourself to recover. Mourning can be a healthy transition only if you don't try to punish yourself in its expression. Don't hide from your memories and strong feelings. Tell them to people who understand, but don't get morbid. Find out where they are in your area, and go to pet bereavement group-support sessions.

10. As soon as you can, talk to your veterinarian. Make a list, in advance, of any questions or doubts you may have about your pet's death. This will prevent forgetting items while you are experiencing strong emotions. It should clear up any possible doubts about everything.

    Such a meeting should be warm and informational. Do not abuse it as a means to get at your pet's doctor. This will also help you to avoid placing unreasonable anger or blame on the veterinarian later. Ask his or her advice, explaining what your bereavement has been like so far. Veterinarians have had considerable experience with other clients who have been through this, and may be able to offer you some practical information as well. Usually, most veterinarians try to stay clear of individual bereavements unless they are asked for advice.

11. Unless there is an emergency, avoid the administration

of euthanasia on special calendar dates that could be up-setting in the future. Prevent yourself from linking bad associations with good ones.

12. Understand and respect your own mourning. If your grief is intense, take some time off from work. Tell your employer that there has been a death in your immediate family. This certainly is true. Most employers provide a specific brief leave for this. Don't try to explain or give excuses. Even if you are prodded to say who died, you don't have to tell. Be firm and insistent, but not con-frontational. Assert yourself at this time. You deserve it. If you can't get any time off, at least you tried. Most likely, you will be respected for this, not criticized.

13. When you are ready, visit an animal shelter to look around, not adopt. You have to be firm with yourself about this. It will help you in many ways if you write down your feelings after this visit, and read them again later. What new thoughts are stimulated by this visit? Don't give in to any sudden impulses to adopt on the spot any of the animals you saw there. If such a response remains with you, go back a second time, and see if you still feel that way. With such feelings, maybe the time is now right.

14. Hold some sort of private service for your beloved pet. You will keep good, permanent remembrances of this. Only friends and family who would appreciate such a ceremony should be invited. Children definitely should be helped to feel they are a basic part of the family in planning and carrying out such a ceremony. This is a very positive activity that has proven to be one of the healthiest beginnings of the mourning process. Such a private service will help you understand your underlying feelings, with a dignity and pride you probably couldn't have appreciated before.

   It need not be of any traditional religious nature. Its purpose is to express your personal spiritual values in a loving retrospective. A few personal words from each person present, followed by your eulogy, should be sufficient. That is up to you. This will almost assuredly get you started through the worst parts of your grief and healing process. Even if you are the only person present, such a ceremony will enrich you and your loving memories.

15. Keep a daily log or journal. List your major thoughts and feelings, but keep it brief. If you feel you want to write at length on the subject, do it separately. Perhaps that could be the basis for an interesting magazine article, essay or short story. Once each day's log is entered, don't change anything. Such a journal will become a treasured part of your memorial to your pet. It will also be of great personal value to you in gaining insight and objectivity into your own thoughts and feelings.

16. Make a list of the things your pet did that used to make you laugh or smile. Add to it as often as you can, even if it takes weeks. Review the items. When you can share these good memories, laughs and tears, read the list to someone who knew the pet and has been supportive during your mourning.

   This positive oasis of loving smiles during your bereavement is part of your healing. It is good medicine. Despite some tears, you will be happier and stronger after each reading of the list. Put it away and keep it forever, along with photographs and other memorabilia that you treasure.

Kitten Mummy: Egyptian, Ptolemaic-Roman; Linen; Height: 20.5 cm., Width: 4.5 cm., Max depth: 6 cm.　　　*Hay Collection, Gift of Granville Way, Courtesy, Museum of Fine Arts, Boston*

154

I.A.P.C.

The following member list has been provided through the courtesy of the International Association of Pet Cemeteries, 2845 Oakcrest Place, Land O'Lakes, FL 34639, (800) 952-5541, founded by Patricia Blosser, in 1971.

"As part of the pet owning public, we each have also grieved the loss of a pet. As I.A.P.C. members, our purpose is to help other people and their family pet member, by providing sincere, realistic pet 'after care' options."

Sincerely,
The Members of the International Association of Pet Cemeteries
Carolyn Kinsey-Shea
Executive Director

AA Sorrento Valley Pet Cemetery and Crematory, Encinitas, CA
AAA Pet Cemetery, Taylor, MI
Abbey Glen Pet Memorial Park, Warren, NJ
Abbingdon Hill Pet Animal Cemetery & Crematory, Montgomery, NY
Alabama Pet Cemetery, Inc., Birmingham, AL
Angel Refuge Pet Cemetery & Crematory, Inc., Mansfield, OH
Angel View Pet Cemetery/Crematory, Middleboro, MA

The Animal Memorial Cemetery & Crematorium, Berkshire Park, New
    South Wales, Australia
Atlanta Pet Cemetery & Crematory, Atlanta, GA
Balmoral Pet Cemetery, Gaylordsville, CT
Beaver Falls Cemetery Memorial Park, Inc., McKeesport, PA
Broward Pet Cemetery, Inc., Plantation, FL
Bubbling Well Pet Memorial Park, Napa, CA
Country Club Pet Memorial Park, Calgary, Alberta, Canada
Dearest Pet Memorial Cemetery, Manahawkin, NJ
Deceased Pet Care Memorial Gardens & Crematory, Duluth, GA
Drownwood National Pet Cemetery, Ellenburg Depot, NY
Dulaney Pet Haven, Timonium, MD
Evergreen Pet Cemetery, Ashland, VA
Evergreen Pet Cemetery & Crematory, Evergreen, CO
Faithful Friends Pet Cemetery, Sandston, VA
Faithful Pets Memorial Gardens, Uniontown, PA
Forest Rest Memorial Park, Glastonbury, CT
Foresthaven Pet Memorial Gardens, Xenia, OH
Forrest Run Pet Cemetery, Menasha, WI
Friendship Pet Memorial Park, Waldorf, MD
Garden of Love Pet Memorial Park, Micanopy, FL
Garden of the Pines Pet Memorial, Virginia Beach, VA
God's Helping Hands, Richmond, MN
Goldren Crates Funeral Home, Findlay, OH
Great Valley Pet Cemetery, Frazer, PA
Greenbriar Pet Cemetery, Auburn, NY
Greenbriar Memory Gardens & Crematory for Pets, Apopka, FL
Harperlawn Pet Memorial Gardens, St. Clair Shores, MI
Hartsdale Canine Cemetery, Hartsdale, NY
Hearthside Rest Pet Cemetery, Erie, PA
Heavenly Acres Pet Cemetery, Howell, MI
Hinsdale Animal Cemetery, Willowbrook, IL
Jancy Pet Cemetery, Zellwood, FL
Katy's Pet Burial Supplies, Cemetery and Crematory, Pekin, IL
Keystone Memorial Park, Bethany, CT
Kimberly Memorial Park, Fogelsville, PA
Lacey Memorial Family Pet Cemetery and Crematory, Hazelton, PA
Lengeman Pet Cemetery, Humane Society of Rochester, NY, Fairport,
    NY
Los Angeles Pet Memorial Park (S.O.P.H.I.E., Inc.), Calabasas, CA

Memory Gardens Cemetery for Pets, Indianapolis, IN
Midwest Cremation Service of Wisconsin, Poynette, WI
Mount Rose Cemetery (Brookside Pet Cemetery), York, PA
My Pet Memorial Park, Utica, NY
Noah's Ark Pet Cemetery, Falls Church, VA
Noah's Garden of Pets, York, PA
Noah's Gardens Pet Cemetery/Mortuary, Grand Rapids, MI
Oakcrest Pet Cemetery and Crematory, Land O'Lakes, FL
Oaklawn Pet Cemetery, Humane Society of Greater Miami, Miami, FL
Paradise Pet Cemetery, Augusta, GA
Paw Print Gardens, West Chicago, IL
Paws Awhile Pet Memorial Park, Inc., Richfield, OH
Peaceful Hills Pet Cemetery, Hartford, WI
Peninsula Pet Rest Cemetery, Newport News, VA
Pet Haven Cemetery, Chattanooga, TN
Pet Haven Cemetery, Kent, WA
Pet Haven Cemetery, Syracuse, NY
Pet Heaven Memorial Park, Miami, FL
Petland, Frederick, MD
Petland Cemetery, Crematory, and Funeral Home, Vineland, NJ
Pet Lawn Cemetery/Crematory, Elmhurst, IL
Pet Lawn Cemetery and Crematory, Milwaukee, WI
Pet Lawn Memorial Park Cemetery and Crematory, Berlin, NJ
Pet Memorial Park, Foxboro, MA
Pet Paradise Cemetery, Jackson, MS
Pet Rest Gardens, Flushing, MI
Pet Rest Memorial Gardens, Marietta, OH
Pet Rest Memorial Park, Watsontown, PA
Pets Rest Cemetery and Crematory, Colma, CA
Pine Rest Pet Cemetery, Inc., West Seneca, NY
Pine Ridge Pet Cemetery, Dedham, MA
Pine View Pet Cemetery, State College, PA
Pinellas Memorial Pet Cemetery and Crematory, Pinellas Park, FL
Pines Pet Cemetery, Lebanon, OH
Pleasant Plains Pet Crematory, Warren, NJ
Precious Pets Cemetery/Crematory, Spencer, OK
Rolling Acres Pet Cemetery, Crematory, Funeral Home and Gift Shop,
    Lincoln, NE
Rosa Bonheur Memorial Park, Baltimore, MD
Royal Oak Pet Cemetery, Brookville, OH

Rush Inter Pet Cemetery and Crematory, West Rush, NY
Sacramento Pet Cemetery and Crematory, Sacramento, CA
Sandy Ridge Pet Cemetery, Eden, Ontario, Canada
Sierra Hills Pet Cemetery, Sacramento, CA
Silver Trails Cemetery and Trails End Crematory, West Brook, CT
S.O.P.H.I.E., Inc. (See Los Angeles Pet Memorial Park)
Suburban Pet Crematory, Cleveland, OH
Sugarloaf Pet Gardens, Barnesville, MD
Sunland Pet Rest, Sun City, AZ
Toothacres Pet Care Center, Carrollton, TX
Tully's Pet Cemetery, Omaha, NE
Valley of the Temples Corp., Kaneohe, HI
Valley Pet Cemetery/Crematory, Williamsport, MD
Valley Pet Memorial Gardens, Kaneohe, HI
West Richfield Country Burial and Cremation, Richfield, OH
Woodside Pet Cemetery, Navarre, OH

Glossary of Terms

ABERRATION—Deviation from normal mental activity or some standard.

ALIENATION—Disappointment, leading to withdrawal or diverting of affections or feelings.

ANTHROPOMORPHIZE—To interpret nonhuman things in terms of human characteristics.

APATHY—The absence or lack of feeling, emotion or caring.

ARRESTED—Stopped, halted progress or normal functioning.

BATTERED—Subjected to strong or overwhelming attack, not necessarily physical.

BEREAVEMENT—The emotional state of being deprived of a loved one because of death.

BLOCK OUT—To not be able to recall something because of related emotional stress.

BONDING—Emotional attachment.

COLUMBARIUM—A vault or special repository for storing the ashes of cremated bodies.

COMPENSATE—To make amends, an adjustment, or supply an equivalent need.

CONDITIONED—Developed or modified by frequent usage or practice.

CONSTRUCT (n)—An object of thought created by the ordering or systematic uniting of elements. An intellectual or logical construction or operational concept.

CREMAINS—The ashes of a body after cremation.

DEFENSE MECHANISM—A psychological reaction in which one defends oneself emotionally.

DEPRESSION—A mental state characterized by very low spirits, sadness and feelings of inadequacy.

DYSFUNCTION—Impaired or abnormal functioning.

ETHOLOGIST—A person who studies the behavior of animals.

EUPHEMISM—The substitution of an agreeable word or phrase for one that is unpleasant.

EVOLVED—Gradually changed or transformed for the better; adapted over a period of time to progressive development or evolution.

EXISTENTIAL—Dealing with existence and being.

FALLIBLE—Capable of error or misperception.

FANTASY—A pleasant mental image created by the imagination to satisfy some need.

GUT FEELING—An extremely subjective, intuitive, personal response or appraisal, lacking suitable explanation, yet profound in its effect on an individual.

HUMANE—An attitude marked by compassion, sympathy and consideration for other beings.

HUMANIST—A person marked by compassion, respect and strong interest in others.

INHERENT—Belonging by nature or settled habit.

JUDGMENTAL—Of or relating to judgment or criticism arising from a personal point of view.

JUSTIFICATION—Vindication or proof of usefulness; explanation or grounds for defending an action or behavior.

MAUDLIN—Gloomily tearful; miserable or excessively sentimental.

METAMORPHOSIS—A stage of growth in transition to higher development.

METAPHOR—A word or phrase used to imply a comparison or separate concept.

MIND-SET—An attitude of being close-minded, opinionated, or having a preconceived set of ideas or views on a subject.

MISPERCEPTION—The incorrect understanding or seeing of an idea.

MORBIDITY—A state of intense misery, discomfort and pain, resulting from disease or upset.

MORES—The morally binding customs or traditions of an established society.

MORTALITY—Fatality caused by a disease, drug or action.

MORTUARY—A business dealing with death and burial.

NEUROTIC—Describing a personal pattern of behavior caused by conflict and insecurity, and marked by tension.

OBJECTIVE (adj)—Clear; able to make an independent appraisal of an idea or situation without being affected by personal feelings or prejudices.

OBSESSIVE—Excessive in some interest or repeated action, sometimes to the point of abnormality.

OSSUARY—A vault or receptacle for the bones/ashes of the dead.

PARADOXICAL—At first, seemingly contradictory or opposed to logic, yet valid.

PATHOLOGICAL—Unhealthy; damaging to physical or mental well-being.

PERCEPTION—Individual awareness or intuitive recognition, insight or intellectual grasp.

PERSPECTIVE—A view of a whole entity in relation and proportion to all its parts.

POST-TRAUMATIC STRESS—Exceptional stress that is caused by a severe emotional shock.

PROGNOSIS—The foretelling of how a condition or disease will change over time.

REPRESS—To exclude from conscious awareness.

ROLE MODEL—A person one looks up to and imitates.

SECONDARY ANGER—The release of pent-up anger, which is triggered by a completely different stimulus not meriting this response.

SELF-DEFEATISM—The act of defeating one's own purposes by unconsciously sabotaging what is thought or done.

SELF-RECRIMINATION—The act of accusing or blaming one's self.

SENTIENT—Aware; consciously perceiving, thinking, feeling.

SEPARATION ANXIETY—Anxiety or distress caused by death or separation.

SLAUGHTERHOUSE REFORM—Social reform to pass laws to remedy the horrible and inhumane conditions in slaughterhouses.

STIMULI—Things that rouse the body, mind or feelings.

SUBCONSCIOUS—The function of the brain in which mental processes take place just below an immediate level of awareness.

SUBJECTIVE—Describing a particular individual's perception, which is modified by personal bias and limitations.

SUPPRESS—To exclude or inhibit from conscious thought or feeling.

SURROGATE—A substitute.

SYMBIOTIC—The positive mutual relationship of two dissimilar organisms, in which each helps the other in some way.

SYMBOL—Anything that suggests or associates other things or ideas.

SYNDROME—A group of related symptoms, collectively typical of a particular problem.

TACTILE CONTACT—Physical contact by touching and feeling.

THERAPEUTIC—Having to do with remedial treatment of a disease.

TLC—Tender loving care.

TRANSCENDENCE—The going beyond usual spiritual limits; excelling, surpassing.

TRAUMA—A state or condition of physical, mental or emotional shock, produced by extreme stress or injury. Emotional stress or blow that may produce disordered feelings or behavior.

TRIGGER MECHANISM—A stimulus that acts as a psychological trigger, suddenly releasing other unrelated responses.

UNCONSCIOUS—That function of the mind which operates completely beyond the levels of awareness.

VENTING—Providing an escape for the release of pressure or suppressed feelings.

VULNERABLE—Open to attack or possible damage; not defensive.

162

About the Author

For the past fourteen years, Wallace Sife, Ph.D., has been in the private practice of psychotherapy, specializing in biofeedback and behavior modification. He has also trained and counseled in human bereavement. Since the untimely death of his own beloved miniature Dachshund, Edel Meister, Dr. Sife has made a dedicated change in the direction of his life, as well as his career. Now he works extensively, in private session and group, with bereaved New Yorkers, who are just learning that there is professional help available for them and their special grief.

Dr. Sife has lectured and given seminars on pet bereavement and euthanasia. He participates in local support groups, and took part in the filming of a TV veterinary series for PBS, dealing with pet bereavement and euthanasia. He helped plan some of the Pace University Annual Pets and People Conferences, and is preparing a future seminar in pet bereavement.

In addition to several other professional and personal affiliations, Dr. Sife is a member of the Delta Society, American Psychological Association, Biofeedback Society, Association for Thanatology, and is the founder and current president of the Association for Pet Bereavement, organized with the enthusiastic participation of several of his pet bereavement patients. He is an active member of the Dachshund Association of Long Island, and has been a successful breeder-owner-handler of miniature Dachshunds. For the past decade, Dr. Sife has also counseled on problem behavior in dogs. His section on comments, advice and responses to letters from members appeared as a regular feature in the bimonthly publication of the original Owner Handlers Association.

This book on pet bereavement is lovingly dedicated to the memory of Dr. Sife's deceased dog, Edel Meister, CD, and all other similarly loved pets through history. He now lives with his two adored miniature Dachshunds, Sheeba and her son, Pip.